you
@work

David R. Baumgartner
Robert (Bo) Brabo
Ann Brown
Jennifer P. Brown
Wendi E. Eldh
Randi Frank
Belinda Goodrich
Michele Fantt Harris
Alicia K. Lambert
Marissa Levin
Nancy Little, PhD
Karl Richter
Lisa Seay
Michele Lawlis Shelton
Tracy Stuckrath

Unlocking Human Potential in the Workplace
A Collection of Insights from Leading HR and OD Experts

Contributing Authors:

David R. Baumgartner Alicia K. Lambert
Robert (Bo) Brabo Marissa Levin
Ann Brown Nancy Little, PhD
Jennifer P. Brown Karl Richter
Wendi E. Eldh Lisa Seay
Randi Frank Michele Lawlis Shelton
Belinda Goodrich Tracy Stuckrath
Michele Fantt Harris

Editing by:
Barb Cahoon Wang
Kate Colbert

Coordinating Editor & Guest Publisher:
Cathy Fyock

Cover design and typesetting by:
Courtney Hudson

First edition, May 2018

You@Work is the third volume in the @Work Series from
Silver Tree Publishing, in collaboration with Cathy Fyock, LLC.

ISBN: 978-1-948238-00-7

Library of Congress Control Number: 2018942326

Created in the United States of America

you
@work

SILVER TREE
PUBLISHING

Table of Contents

Acknowledgments
from the Publishers

It is with great respect and gratitude that we acknowledge the authors who have contributed to this anthology. We value the faith that each has placed in us, and we are honored by the association with such esteemed and talented professionals. Our 15 amazing authors shared highly personal stories and insights, as well as detailed frameworks and strategies, about what it means — for organizations, for individuals and for teams — when we bring our true selves to the workplace. As we worked together to produce this anthology, we demonstrated through our actions the true spirit of unlocking human potential for the greater good. We laughed and we learned; we embraced each other's differing perspectives; we questioned the status quo; and we believe in one another and in the power of this book to do good in the world.

Working with these authors, whose credentials and experiences will wow you and inspire you, was like receiving a gift. They reminded us that every employee matters, every day; that we grow in our jobs and our careers by being our most authentic selves; and that great organizations and great teams are, at their essence, a magical collection of great leaders and great employees.

Throughout the authoring and publishing process of *You@Work*, we had the chance to get to know each author as an individual — and the vision for this collection was put to work as we celebrated the power of individuality in the context of shared business objectives. The powerful stories, keen insights and important practical advice of these 15 authors were universally shared with enthusiasm, professionalism and, most important, a compassionate sense of humanity. It has been a privilege to work with them all.

We also would like to extend our gratitude to Sharon Armstrong of the SAA Trainers and Consultants Network, a free referral service for HR, OD, trainers, coaches, and keynote speakers. Sharon is an HR consultant and author who was very helpful to us as we set out to develop this anthology. She can be reached at 202-333-0644 or online at www.trainersandconsultants.net.

With the underlying theme of individuality and humanity at work, this anthology demonstrates the breadth of ways you and your organization can unlock human potential in the workplace by looking within — within ourselves and within one another. By sharing their stories, these authors show practical and accessible ways that Human Resources, chief executives and other professionals can employ, teach and support the value of placing compassion and concern for the individual employee at the heart of the workplace. We are proud to share their experiences and important insights with you. We hope you will share what *you* learn from this collection with others.

– Kate Colbert and Cathy Fyock

Chapter One

DAVID R. BAUMGARTNER

"You@Work – Know You or No You"

In 1993, I was self-employed and trying to find an easy way to get through the day. One night I started reading M. Scott Peck's best seller, *The Road Less Traveled*. The first chapter hit me like a ton of rocks. I was forever and profoundly changed at work and ultimately in my personal life. To paraphrase, Peck says that life is difficult, and that when you realize and accept that life is difficult, and learn to deal with those difficulties, life suddenly becomes surprisingly easy.

Was difficulty the story of my life to that point?! At work, people were always calling because they wanted something. Sometimes it was small things going wrong in their world, causing them heartburn, and sometimes there were issues with the service I or one of our team members was providing. At home, we had three children under the age of 10, and my wife and I were on the back side of two years of marriage counseling because our seven-year-itch had become a major rash. I remember my mindset was "problems everywhere!"

When you realize and accept that life is difficult, and learn to deal with those difficulties, life suddenly becomes surprisingly easy.

Reading Peck's first chapter, it dawned on me that if life is difficult for *everyone* (and not only for me), I could be in demand if I embraced that concept at work and reached out with solutions. From then on, my perspective for noticing unexpected issues at work became an opportunity to be a problem-solver. Over my career, having that mindset and mission at work hasn't failed me!

Unfortunately, it was probably 20 more years before I truly embraced and connected these concepts in my personal life. While I have had relative success at work, real success didn't happen until I connected my work and personal lives. Connecting these two integral halves of life has been a journey that ultimately has brought real peace to me, and I hope it can have the same impact for you too.

Through this journey of discovery, four overarching life lessons emerged that helped me make the vital connection:

- **Chill Out**: Dealing with Frustration
- **Sorry, It's Not About You**: Accepting Responsibility for Yourself
- **Having the Long View**: Learning Patience
- **Embrace Your Bias**: Yesterday and Tomorrow

While my journey in getting to know myself isn't like others, the lessons are universal and can benefit anyone. In my opinion, the sooner these lessons are learned and accepted, the better. Until I got to know "me" at work, there could be no "me." This is the understanding I needed in order to give everything of myself to others in a humble, confident way.

In this chapter, I'll explore each of these lessons in terms of connecting the work "you" and the personal "you."

Chill Out: Dealing with Frustration

_____

"It would not be life if there were not temporality involved, which is sorrow — loss. You've got to say yes to life and see it as magnificent this way; for this is surely the way God intended it."

– Joseph Campbell, *The Power of Myth*

Frustration is that gnawing feeling we have when something isn't going as expected. In general, it could be the behavior of others gnawing on us: family, friends, colleagues, subordinates, supervisors, politicians, clergy, teachers. The list can go on and on.

At work, it could be the job itself begging us to answer questions: "Is this work appealing?" or "Why is this my job?" And your answer might be:

- Because of the money/title.

- Because it's all that is available.

- Maybe it's the job that a 50-year-old adult ends up with as a result of his former 18-year-old self having decided, all those years ago, what to study in college.

- Maybe this is a job or role that matches my passions, but it's hard to make a living at it.

Maybe you are having frustrations over your health, athletic ability, appearance, money, possessions or neighborhood. For many of us, our questions and subtle frustrations are many and ever-present.

As mentioned, early in my career I read M. Scott Peck, and his message laid a foundation that served me over the years as I worked primarily in healthcare human resources. I am able to embrace ever-changing conditions with a focus on engaging the frontline caregiver, and I've been blessed to partner with like-minded colleagues to find that balance between regulatory, payment and other restraints with the need to organizationally engage people.

Midway into my career, the mindset of embracing others' frustration as opportunities came to fruition after I achieved Six Sigma Green Belt and learned to practice Lean principles. Asking front line employees about their vocal frustration at work, nine out of 10 times it's not because they are bitter as much as they are frustrated with redundant steps in the job and wasteful efforts. Process improvement training and mindset enables people to get past the emotion of most of the front-line frustration and move into root cause problem-solving.

Later, I had the opportunity to work with corporate, divisional and regional leaders who were frustrated because their teams were struggling. A common theme? The frustration that erupts as a byproduct an inability to truly connect with and build a team around them that supports their vision. Often the bridge to that gap can begin to be built by asking the leaders questions that help them get past the emotional frustration toward identifying the behaviors that were the source of the frustration:

- Tell me about the last three team members who didn't make it.

- Why, and what specifically, did they do that led to their departure?

- Tell me five words that describe you as a person/leader?

    Often, when queried, these leaders would use words like integrity, positive, caring, goal-oriented and team-focused. Then we move forward to get clarity around each of the words and examples of behaviors. "When you started this job and had that first discussion with the team," I ask, "did you tell them this about you?" Often the answer is *no*!

You can begin to see the light bulb go on. Sitting back in their chair, you can tell they would really start thinking when you ask a question. They would highlight a word, and then we could "ice the cake" talking about the behaviors of the last three people who didn't make the team; they would soon realize that most of the reasons were because there was conflict with one of the five words that describe the leader as a person.

For example, one facility CEO recently separated with their organization's Nursing Director because of various reasons, with a major factor being the Nursing Director's inability to connect with his team. Getting to the root of why it didn't work out started with the CEO. So I asked the CEO to provide five words that describe her. She used words like integrity, work ethic, etc., but the one word that stood out was "Joy." My response: "Joy — what does that mean?" The CEO went on to describe how she was a "glass half-full person," seeing the opportunity in everything. After a short discussion, I asked; "so if I'm technically sound in my job yet more negative than optimistic in my disposition, are you and I going to have a hard time working together?" There was a noticeable inquisitive expression om her face. She sat back and said, "Probably."

Then I asked: "You have been in this role for a year. When you had the 1st meeting with your leadership team, what did you tell them about your expectations?" The CEO responded with something like, "I expect you to do your job, focus on quality and our customer …" Hmm. So I asked her, "I noticed you didn't say anything about your *values* — nothing about those five important words that describe you." She believed she didn't need to — that it could go unsaid because she "leads by example." My response? "If these values are so important to you that they may cost me my job in the end, do you think it's fair to leave bread crumbs and hope that your team picks them up?"

Sometimes the big issues at work — the messy, people issues are really communications issues. Often, leaders' source of frustration comes from people on their team conflicting with their important personal beliefs or values. From there, it's a matter of coaching team members to realize what's happening and to learn ways to balance that with reality and the needs of the organization.

Sorry, It's Not About You: Accepting Responsibility for Yourself

----

"In the long run we shape our lives, and we shape ourselves. The process never ends until we die. And the choices we make are ultimately our own responsibility."

– Eleanor Roosevelt

Closely linked to dealing with frustration is the ability to separate your feelings, worth, goals and aspirations from the behavior of others, and to accept responsibility for your own actions. At work, it starts with setting expectations and holding people accountable.

It doesn't matter your level of responsibility. At any level, you must own your behavior.

1. As a team member, just because everyone else does something negative or counter-productive doesn't mean I have to do likewise.

   - Avoid gossip, harsh language or petty policy violations.
   - Know your values without needing the approval of others.
   - Be careful to avoid reality with idealism. Don't give up on values and also check to make sure one's perspective is not jaded.

2. As a team leader, be clear about values and coach people along. In the prior book in the @Work Series, *Compassion@Work*, we explore this topic and The Four Rules a little more.

    – Don't assume people will "get it" just because of a quick conversation.

    – Invest in building alignment.

    – At the end, decide whether separating is the right course of action.

    – Avoid emotion when talking about behavior that conflicts with an expressed value.

Closely linked to dealing with frustration is the ability to separate your feelings, worth, goals and aspirations from the behavior of others, and to accept responsibility for your own actions.

At work, being responsible for one's own behavior is rooted in being able to identify and articulate where you stand. Then you can separate your behavior from others.

In one's personal life, this is significantly harder. However, along the journey of life, being able to truly accept this has been a cornerstone in my journey. We have expectations about the way we believe a parent, spouse, child or friend should act. But how often do others do things that conflict with that expectation?

My parents were into their 70s when my mom filed for divorce. Through that long time-period, my mom disconnected from my family. I went through all the stages of grief from disbelief and ultimately, to acceptance. Wondering how she could do this, I assumed it was something I did or because my family stayed connected with dad. I said to myself, "How can a mother do this?" But at the end of the day, peace came when I was able to accept that all I can control are my own reactions to the difficult things in my life, and to love and accept people who are different from me and make different decisions than I do (sometimes easier said than done!).

I'm not a counselor, so I can't go into detail on this, but the same principle applies to the behavior of children. Teach them to make decisions, allow them to live with their decisions and then let go. People who live with loved ones who have addictions know this all too well.

This doesn't mean, however, that there is not pain or challenge during difficult times. It just means that you can't live the life of another person. Finding peace with this in personal life has been a great foundation for being content with my behavior at work.

Having the Long View: Learning Patience

"You need a very strong container to hold the contents and contradictions that arrive later in life. You ironically need a very strong ego structure to let go of your ego."

 – **Richard Rohr**, *Falling Upward: A Spirituality for the Two Halves of Life*

In my chapter in *Compassion@Work*, I briefly mention a conversation with our oldest daughter when The Four Rules were born. In that conversation, I introduced her to the timeline illustrated below because she was making decisions that a 15-year-old would normally make. In the conversation, I took out a piece of paper and drew two lines representing zero and 40. "Where's 20?" I asked. She pointed, and I drew a line. Continuing, "Where's 14?"

She pointed, and I drew a line." And 18?" She pointed, and
I drew a final vertical line. Bracketing the lines between 14 and
18, I explained, "I'm 40, and at this point in life I routinely talk to
a handful of people I knew when I was in high school — Your age!"
Continuing, I bracketed between the 14 and 18 lines and the 40
vertical line saying, "I know you believe these times and people are
important, but only time will teach you the truth."

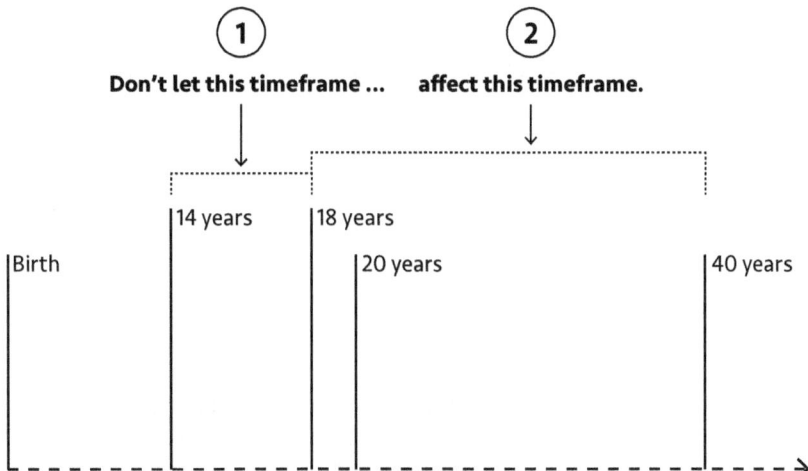

The whole conversation — The Four Rules and the timeline chart
— happened on the fly and lasted about 12 minutes. While I'll
admit I'm not an artist or good with the hand, she got the point,
and it became a tool for teaching all four children to calm down
and think about the long view. It didn't matter if they were talking
about friends or whether this is the right person to get serious
with; time will give you the answer. Be patient.

The reality of having the long view brings calm to short-term frustrations and others' behavior. Knowing the larger mission at work
avoids people getting caught up in tactics. Life and work will never
go exactly as we imagine or plan, but persistence toward the goal/

vision/mission (or what others might call "grit") is a valuable trait that can be acquired.

My guiding principle in life is Steven Covey's Habit #2: Begin with the end in mind. I strive to live each day treating people the way I want them to talk about me at my funeral. Having the long view guides my steps today — being flexible with tactics while staying focused on the long-term goal.

Embrace Your Bias: Yesterday and Tomorrow

"I never considered a difference of opinion in politics, in religion, in philosophy as a cause from withdrawing from a friend."

– Thomas Jefferson

Later in life I took a critical thinking class. It changed my whole perspective on life including how I thought about religion, politics, race and sexual orientation — basically everything. In a nutshell, my past is who I am. I can't do anything about it now. Mistakes — the "what if's," the "should have's," the "what you did to me's" — are all done!

When my kids were growing up and they'd made a decision I had an issue with, after talking about it, they'd realize they could have made a different decision. I'd ask, "Are mistakes good or bad?" They'd respond, "Good, when you learn from them!"

My yesterday, or bias, is the great teacher in life. It enables me to ask questions about today, helping me to try to understand someone or something that is going on. From their use, what I'm learning now guides my steps for tomorrow.

At work, realizing why I think the way I do comes from my past.
I embrace that bias, or perspective, and realize that we all come from
somewhere totally different. Teamwork and synergy comes from the
ability of multiple people to become one. Our collective "now" is the key
for a successful tomorrow.

THE JOURNEY IS A HERO'S JOURNEY

Think about any great story: *The Odyssey*, the original *Star Wars* with Luke
Skywalker. They are all what Joseph Campbell calls a "Hero's Journey."

Life if full of challenges; some are huge — such as job loss, health
concerns, or relationship challenges. We all know some people who are
able to get knocked out of known comfortable territory and go through
some sort of abyss and come out the other side with peace and wisdom
that should be cherished by all those willing to learn.

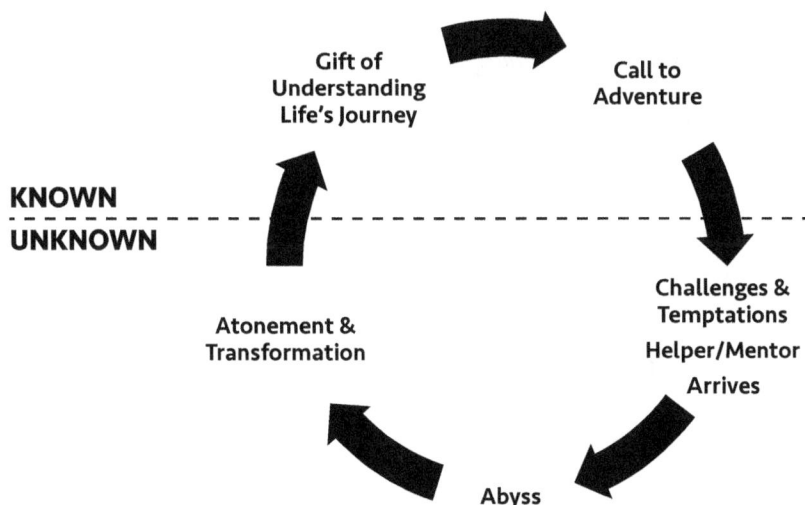

Gift of
Understanding
Life's Journey

Call to
Adventure

KNOWN

UNKNOWN

Challenges &
Temptations
Helper/Mentor
Arrives

Atonement &
Transformation

Abyss

My hypothesis is that the hero's journey certainly contains big challenging journeys and small everyday journeys being confronted with something new. The question is "Will I come through today learning something new, ready to try something different tomorrow to accomplish Odysseus's ultimate goal of getting home?"

Getting to know myself enables "me" to bring "me" to work. It enables me to be fully in control of me so I can stay focused on values and goals that are important to my life's journey. For me, this hasn't happened alone. I've been blessed to have good people coach me along the way and now I have had the opportunity to coach and help others as we learn life together.

Life is full of unexpected turns, which are the challenge and the gift. The challenge is not getting caught up and frustrated with the unexpected but using life as the divine teacher of tomorrow. My past is the way to learn and move forward to a better future, always stay flexible with the tactics in life while staying focused on the long-range vision.

"Life is a wonderful symphony; play it well."

 – Joseph Campbell

ABOUT THE AUTHOR

David R. Baumgartner
SHRM-SCP, SPHR, SSGB, CNA, NPS Certified

With more than 20 years of senior-level HR experience, David has worked with operators to achieve organizational metrics through clearly defined objectives and effective messaging that creates collaborative focus.

David's experience includes working on mergers and acquisitions in various roles. In all such projects, the goal is to align organizational goals to create cultures of highly engaged, customer-focused employees. Because David is dedicated to the role that consumer feedback plays in overall organizational health, he also carries net promoter score (NPS) certification.

David works with and coaches leaders to accomplish operational goals, including improving engagement in an acquired region from worst to top tier, improving divisional leadership scores from worst to first, and improving organizational team focus.

David's current assignment is VP of Spirituality & Sacred Six for Signature Healthcare, where he is part of the group that guides the chaplain team for Signature's 120-plus facilities. He has spoken at healthcare associations at the state and national levels. In addition to his work at Signature, David partners with his wife, Karen, to provide HR consulting on culture and executive coaching services to a small number of organizations and individuals.

David's favorite times are with his wife, children and grandchildren — grillin' and chillin', boating in SC, being in the mountains hiking, golfing or just working on a project around someone's house.

He is thankful for the guidance and support of many friends and colleagues as well as the people at St. Peter Claver in Lexington, KY.

Learn more and contact David:

dbaumgartner@tresane.com

Linkedin.com/in/drbaumgartnerky

Twitter.com/drbaumgartner

Chapter Two

ROBERT (BO) BRABO

"RESPECT: It's a Verb. It's About Behavior. We Can Model Behavior!"

Look up the word "respect" on dictionary.com and you'll find seven definitions listed as a noun and four listed as a verb. The seven nouns should be scratched, and we should solely focus on the verb, the action, the behavior it takes to demonstrate respect. If you've never actually thought about it, other than to say, "Yeah, I show respect to others," then take a journey with me in this chapter. Let's see where it takes us.

I've designed a conceptual model around this topic and it's summarized here to fit in one chapter. The **Bo5 Model** is designed to invoke **ACTION**. It's short, concise and in-your-face like a drill sergeant so you'll remember: Respect is a verb. As you read through, think of the model as a tool set you can employ during your day. The more complicated a tool set is, the less likely we may be to use it, so here it's simple. Read my examples and think of your own experiences to make it real for you.

The Bo5 Model is designed to invoke ACTION. It's short, concise and in-your-face like a drill sergeant so you'll remember: Respect is a verb.

The *Bo*5 Model of Respect

1. **Show Up!**

2. **Sit Up!**

3. **Stand Up!**

4. **Speak Up!**

5. **Shut Up!**

SHOW UP!

If we were to define this in just three words, they'd be "Be on Time." But it's much more than that. Show Up means to be there in the good times and the bad; to bring your A-game every time; to be on time with your work deliverables; to be prepared and on time for meetings; to be focused on the topic at hand. The list goes on.

"How is this respect?" you ask. Consider an example of a meeting that YOU scheduled with your team. You show up 10 minutes late, have no agenda put together, nothing to present, and you didn't communicate the desired goal/outcome of the meeting. Did you demonstrate any respect for your team? Of course not. In fact, your team members left the meeting whispering under their breath or texting each other saying that was a complete waste of their time (and probably a few other expletives as well).

With the ever-popular webinar these days, here's another example that I'm sure we've all experienced and in my humble opinion, it's become commonplace: Regardless of the number of participants that registered for the webinar (really this could be any teleconference or video conference), the organizer welcomes people to the webinar at the scheduled start time and then immediately follows by saying something like, "Let's wait a few minutes as others are still joining the meeting." WHAT??? I showed up on time and now we're waiting! C'mon, I have things to do so let's get this show on the road. Those are my sentiments every time. What's happening is that the organizer is showing respect to the *dis*-respecters and showing *dis*-respect to those who "SHOWED UP"! In the case of the webinar, the script has flipped and we need to right the ship.

Take the meeting set-up rules by Jeff Bezos, CEO of Amazon, as an example. Bezos ensures an agenda for the meeting is sent to participants in advance, as well as agreeing upon the meeting's desired outcomes before the meeting. Then, when the meeting starts, there is a 10 to 15-minute period of silence for participants to read the agenda and the memo that outlines what's to be discussed during the meeting. In case a participant wasn't prepared, Bezos helps them out just a bit in this way to get them ready for discussion. It's a leadership tactic that highlights the "Show Up" nature of respect.

SIT UP!

This is as much about perception as it is about real respect. Envision a meeting with participants seated around a conference room table or even co-workers at their desks. Are they slouches or sliders (slid way down in their chairs)? What thoughts come to mind when you see this?

- Not interested
- Lazy
- Mind is elsewhere
- Not getting their work done
- Not taken seriously
- Don't care
- Etc.

We may have other thoughts as well, but we'll keep those to ourselves. The point here is to be objective about viewing yourself and consider whether this is you or not. If it is, do something about it because, as we've pointed out, we're always being observed by our co-workers (subordinates, peers and superiors alike) and perception is a real thing to deal with.

How do you fix it?

- Sit up in your chair.
- Find a chair that fits you (ergonomics matter).
- Practice good posture.
- In meetings, make eye contact with the person speaking (and this is easier to do when you're sitting up).

A few simple changes and you'll find perception changes at the same time. Now you're a contender; you're present and accounted for; others will listen to you; you're focused; you're showing respect.

Now you're a contender; you're present and accounted for; others will listen to you; you're focused; you're showing respect.

STAND UP!

There are multiple scenarios that occur during the workday where this tool has the potential to elevate you to a different level. First, Stand Up means just that, STAND UP. A physical movement of getting up off your fourth point of contact (Airborne term for buttocks) and standing on your feet. Consider the following and how another person might truly feel you showed them respect with one quick move:

> You are sitting at your desk in your office or at your cubicle, and your boss comes to you to ask a question or give some feedback. At the very moment you know she's there, stand and give her your attention. This will demonstrate your focus and recognition of her authority. The boss will remember you for the respect you showed her. Do it regularly and the boss will know that respect is part of your character. Please take note: This doesn't' have to be a scenario with your boss; it can be applied to anyone.

Now, let's say you are the person who stands and you want to get others to show the same respect. Here's a tip to invoke change on the down-low, because this change is all about behavior and having co-workers follow your lead. When you arrive at a meeting, DO NOT sit down at the table until the leader shows up and sits down. Over time, others will start to see what you're doing and may ask you why, thus giving you an opening to explain, or they may simply follow suit. Worse case, because you're the one standing and no one else is, your respect for the leader will surely be recognized by the leader herself.

SPEAK UP!

Of the five points in the Bo5 Model, this may be the one that's not the easiest to accomplish, especially if you're an introvert and only think of it as verbal speaking in front of others. At work, at home and in life YOU are unique and have ideas, thoughts and feelings — important things that others should hear … or READ. But you must share them.

Let's talk about sharing these important things in a respectful manner. I've used the meeting set-up in previous examples, so I'll build upon that here too. Regardless of the type of meeting (e.g., in-person, teleconference, webinar, etc.), there is a time for each participant to speak. Keeping that in mind, we need to take a step back for just a moment. Meetings have topics or reasons for occurring. Preparation for the meeting is the key to speaking in the meeting. You must take the time to study before attending the meeting and make pre-meeting notes (comments and questions) before ever stepping foot in the meeting. If you happen to be the introvert, this alone will help you gain the confidence to Speak Up during the meeting.

Speak Up also has another connotation regarding others showing YOU respect. For those of you responsible for leading others, do you have their back? Do you *really* have their back? Do you Speak Up on their behalf, or are you the one who takes credit for their work when it's good but throws them under the bus when it's bad? If you're "that person," you're not a leader at all and will never earn their respect. I don't say this here to sound tough, but to invoke self-reflection and to ensure that, if nothing else, any leader reading this understands that those she leads deserve her voice on their behalf. Speak Up, give credit and take the heat!

SHUT UP!

Harsh? I hope so. Just as there's a time to speak, there's also a time to keep your lips in contact with each other. If you've been part of any group meeting, I'd find it hard to believe that you didn't witness people speaking, whispering, gossiping, interrupting or a slew of other things when someone else had the floor. Repetitive behavior like this is *dis*-respect deserving of a trip to the HR Exec's office to discuss employee relations! To be absolutely clear and non-politically correct, Shut Up really does mean Shut Up.

Just as we need to know when to speak up, we need to also recognize when it's time to not speak (more politically correct maybe). Here's a short list of those times:

- Anytime someone else is speaking (or "has the floor," so to say);
- When your comment has nothing to do with the topic;
- When all you have is a joke (it may not be funny or appropriate to all);
- When you're speaking just to hear yourself speak (demonstrating arrogance versus respect)
- Etc.

Have you ever been somewhere, say a restaurant or movie theater and someone's phone rings, and then they sit right there and take the call? I imagine that you have had this experience, as I have, and it has a tendency to stir up a certain level of anger within us. The person taking the call is showing their narcissistic, disrespectful self to the world around them. Now, what about a similar scenario during a meeting at work? The person who did that at the restaurant will do it in the meeting too. The solution may be obvious to most but needs to be said anyway: If your phone must be on during a meeting and a call comes in (hopefully it's on vibrate or silent), you have two choices to show respect for those around you: 1) Let the call go to voicemail and deal with it later, or 2) Pick up your phone, leave the meeting and take the call in private elsewhere. Others in the meeting will see your respect and appreciate your actions.

Sidebar conversations are another example of disrespecting the speaker, and it happens regularly. The disruption or annoyance for those hearing the sidebar, or even for the speaker, is much like the heckler to a comedian on stage. It throws off concentration and focus, and has the potential to derail the entire flow of the meeting. What to do? If you're the sidebar talker or heckler as I'll call you, you need to learn how to zip it; if what you have to say is relevant, share it with the group when it's your time to speak. If it's super important at that moment, take a play from the schoolhouse classroom and raise your hand ... that, folks, is showing respect.

There it is, the Bo5 Model of Respect (Show Up, Sit Up, Stand Up, Speak Up and Shut Up) summarized in a short chapter. After 20 years on active duty in the US Army and 10 years in private industry, I've witnessed the good, the bad and the ugly when it comes to demonstrating respect. Through our actions, we are fully capable of generating feelings, emotions and even modeling good behavior in others. Respect, much like love, is empty without the right behaviors to back it up. It truly is my opinion that this word should only exist as an actionable concept, and if we do our best to employ this model and show respect to ALL others as a regular part of our lives, we would change the world ... one respectful action at a time!

ABOUT THE AUTHOR

Robert (Bo) Brabo
PMP, SPHR

Bo Brabo has a combined 30 years of human resource management experience in the Department of Defense and private industry. Shortly after retiring from the U.S. Army as the Director of HR Operations for the White House Communications Agency, Bo co-founded Brabo West, Inc., with a long-time mentor of his. The company, situated in the Washington, DC, metro area, focuses on recruiting, HR consulting, finance and accounting for clients primarily involved in government contracting.

Recently, Bo had an opportunity to jump into the healthcare industry; and joined Advantia Health LLC as their head of HR. What intrigued Bo about the company was the leadership vision and opportunity to participate heavily in fast growth via acquisition, requiring Bo's simultaneous HR, project management and people skills to integrate systems and significant numbers of employees.

During his eight years at the White House Communications Agency, Bo had an additional duty as a Presidential Communications Officer. He was trained and certified to lead communication teams to deliver direct support to both Presidents Bush and Obama. Having stood with each President in the

Oval Office, Bo uses his experience to encourage and mentor others to dream big and reach for the stars!

Bo holds a bachelor's degree in business administration and is a current candidate in the Executive MBA program at the University of Michigan Ross School of Business.

Learn more and contact Bo:

rbrabo@brabowest.com

BraboWest.com

LinkedIn.com/in/RobertBrabo

Chapter Three

ANN BROWN

"Take Care of the Ecosystem, Like a Gardener"

Have you ever started a new position and wondered how you would become part of an existing team and hit the ground running? Have you ever been in a position to lead a cross-functional project or a team and wondered how you were going to utilize all the talent on the team and reach the goals? If you answered "yes" to hitting the ground running, leading, and then jumped right to the goal, come on and dig into this chapter. You, my friend, have found your tribe. #GetStuffDone

Let's do a quick level-set about leadership and culture first. Anyone can lead from where they are, even without a leadership title, if they choose to do so. While leadership is unique to everyone, there are some common ways to define the term as found in multiple leadership books and the internet. When I work with teams, I have found that I must:

- Get to know the people and the customers we serve;
- Ask questions to gain clarity and explore beliefs;
- Explore options, even things not tried before;
- Inspire teammates to act or opt-in; and

- Create space for the team to accomplish goals and, in many cases, make things better.

Hanging our hat on this final idea of "creating space," let's look at culture as well. While engagement and culture are often used interchangeably, they are quite different. Culture is the thing that shows up in the room when no one is looking. The behaviors, motivators and work styles of the team define culture, whereas personal feelings about a thing define engagement. Culture is created, measured and enhanced from the "we" perspective, while engagement looks at the "I" perspective.

Culture is the thing that shows up in the room when no one is looking.

How team members feel about their work can easily be affected by temporary climate factors, such as an office move, a challenging project or organizational change. These factors and our feelings about them can change weekly, daily and even hourly. Culture, on the other hand, are those deeply engrained behavior norms.

Every cross-functional or department team has a culture. And yes, this could be a different culture from the overall organizational culture. Taking care to intentionally form culture is critical to developing, growing and retaining talent. When the culture is strong, it will quickly spit out things that go against it. A strong culture won't let things linger because what people believe, say and do are all in line. People bring themselves *into* the culture instead of taking from it.

THE JOURNEY

A few years ago, a team I lead was faced with the typical and necessary phases of team evolution or development: forming, storming, norming and performing.[1] Each of the four stages builds upon the previous stage, and ultimately prepares the group for performing. Of course, the impatient side of me wanted to quickly move through the first two phases so we could get to norming and performing. After all, we had a lot to accomplish because the organization was in the middle of working through several large, continuous improvement events and was prioritizing change; they needed us to start *and* complete many things, including a curriculum overhaul.

Several new team members joined us during this time as well. So, this could be called "The Perfect Storm." Why? Well, when you mix the demands of caring for people with aligning to business needs changing at an extremely fast pace, developing our change management strategy across the organization, increasing learning scalability for a dispersed and growing organization, and adding new positions and personalities to the team, that equals fun times, my friend.

So, what comes first? The work or the people? Is there time for both to be first? The answer is "yes," and you *must* take care of the people to accomplish the work. People do a lot more than accomplish work. They are smart and often bring diverse talents to the workplace; they have experiences they want to share; and they want to be included in solving the organization's problems. After all, they choose to work there and are often committed to positive outcomes to move the organization

---

1   This often-cited team development model was first proposed by Dr. Bruce Tuckman n 1965.

forward. They also have feelings and needs, and often simply want to be included. #IncludeMe

That little nugget above I learned after being in the storming phase longer than I would have liked. Remember the part about me being impatient? Experience is a wonderful teacher; if you choose to be the student and decide to make a different choice next time, you have a similar opportunity.

So, back to my dilemma: How could I get this team of extremely talented and passionate professionals to pull together *and* quickly move through the storming phase? Well, invite them to be part of the process to establish the team's culture, of course. Seriously, I had two options — tell them to stop storming or invite them to stop, collaborate and listen to each other.

WHEN #INCLUDEME AND #GETSTUFFDONE MEET, GREAT THINGS CAN HAPPEN

After several weeks of storming, my heart couldn't take the emotions of this phase anymore. This was keeping us all up at night. At our next team meeting, we simply focused on us. I led the team through an activity, "The Idea of a Perfect Team."

Armed with flipchart paper, black Sharpies® and Post-It® notes, we started imagining the characteristics and environment of a perfect team. Each person wrote all their thoughts and ideas on sticky notes and filled the "basket" of a perfect team. It was important that we all participated and that every thought was explored. After all, we were exploring personal beliefs, defining our team's values and, ultimately, building the culture.

We worked as a team to create an affinity diagram. The process was simple, like the picture below. First, we captured all the ideas, opinions and issues listed on the Post-It notes. Then we read, sorted and grouped similar items together. Finally, we labeled each group of notes with natural relationship headings, such as trust, respectful behaviors, listening, inclusion, standard work processes, etc.

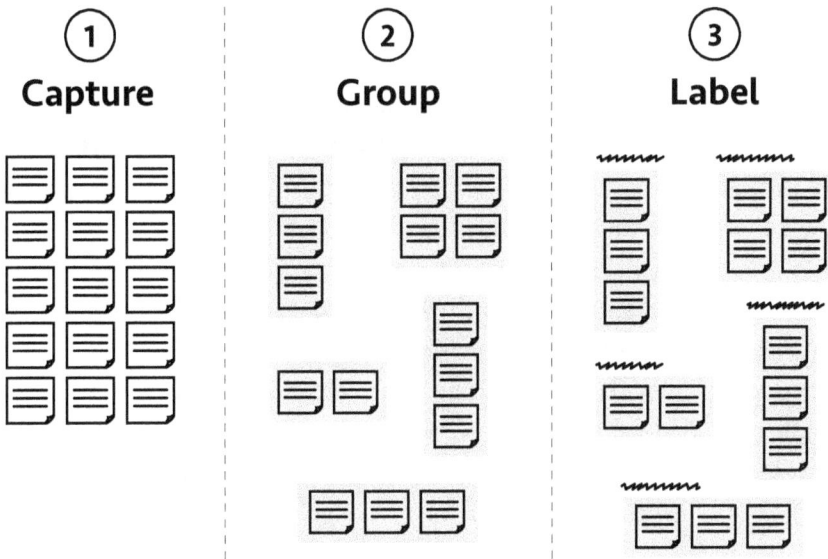

① Capture   **② Group**   **③ Label**

The outcomes of this exercise were significant, as it created space for everyone to lead on the team, be accountable for their own actions and how they were impacting the team, and hold others accountable. After a few revisions to the labels that denoted behaviors, we realized our team values were closely aligned with The Basic Principles and Team Qualities training content from Achieve Global.

1. Focus on the situation, issue or behavior, not on the person.

2. Maintain the self-confidence and self-esteem of others.

3. Maintain constructive relationships.

4. Take initiative to make things better.

5. Lead by example.

6. Think beyond the moment.

MORE STOPS ON THE JOURNEY

We had momentum going and became intentional about checking in frequently to examine what was going well and to discuss soft spots. This allowed us to listen to each other, and authentic relationships started to form and grow. As we checked, adjusted and kept moving forward, we also co-created our team's mission statement. We answered questions such as: Why do we exist? How do we add value to the organization?

Remember, the organization *and* our team were growing. We had to take care and protect what we were building while getting stuff done. We examined our commitments as individuals to keep the team pulling together while aligning to business needs and changes. We also co-created how we would hire and integrate new team members into our high-performing team.

"Blessed are the flexible, for they shall not get bent out of shape."

– Unknown

What we were building had to continue evolving. We were becoming a family and we had to continuously invest in *us* so that we could be cohesive and support our customers. We watched videos, read books, attended classes, did various team-building outings, built trust, and learned to have meaningful two-way dialogue and how to fight fair. No, there were no physical fights and we never came close to that. Because we are adults, we come to the workplace with different experiences and different levels of skill sets on how to develop and maintain healthy relationships.

As I continued to scan what was going on in the organization and in my team, I knew we had accomplished a lot and still had more things to do. Timelines and deadlines were not slowing down, even when "life" happened. Our team's skill sets needed to evolve as well so that eLearning, videos, facilitation, project management, change management or other work didn't pile up on one person's plate. We again worked together to learn new skills that included more efficient approaches to our work, and we continued balancing priorities as a team and as individuals.

Working together and co-creating along the way is one of the secrets to a high-performing team. This intentional inclusion is important to unlocking human potential anywhere, really. During one of our team outings, we went to an escape room where we had 60 minutes to work together to find clues, solve puzzles and get out. We escaped the room at the 59-minute and 55-second mark (59:55). This is important as it became our mantra and continues to this day. Time grounds us in remembering to trust and respect each other as we divide and conquer to successfully accomplish things and move forward.

Working together and co-creating along the way is one of the secrets to a high-performing team. This intentional inclusion is important to unlocking human potential anywhere, really.

FOR SUCH A TIME AS THIS

At that time, I didn't realize just how important the time we spent building the team culture would be for me, my team and the organization. I was simply leading with my heart and passion for growing and developing others to make meaningful impacts. I knew we could do great things. I simply never imagined how much our work and personal lives would intersect.

Suddenly, life started happening to most people on my team, including me. It felt like the worst timing on several fronts: 1. we were simply exhausted and didn't want to experience it, and 2. we were in the midst of several large "all-hands-on-deck projects." One of the joys of being human is that we are always at choice — stall out or keep going.

"Never give up. Today is hard, tomorrow will be worse, but the day after tomorrow will be sunshine."

– Jack Ma

For a while, every couple of months someone was out on leave, experienced a sudden loss of a loved one, or dealt with life-changing surgeries and even cancer. We joked about having a full team, finally, on the odd days that this occurred. We experienced four team members out on leave and hired and onboarded two new team members in a 12-month time-span. Not only do I remain amazed at how the team didn't miss a beat — including delivering on unforeseen needs — the love and care they had for me and for each other was incredible.

Suddenly, I needed to be out on leave as well. When I shared this unexpected news with the team, I was immediately showered with their concern and support. We had about three weeks to prepare for my departure; however, that really wasn't an issue. Because I was intentional about collaboration and because they began connecting with stakeholders early on, they were already working on and leading key work streams on organizational projects. I simply wrapped up the part of my to-do list that I could and worked to remove any hurdles that were in their way.

The support didn't stop with my team though. My leader, peers and others in the organization offered to help in any way they could — inside and outside of work. Multiple people were praying with us and for us. On my last day, I was brought to tears during multiple acts of kindness. From a team prayer to discovering such thoughtful and unexpected gifts in a care package for my family, including daily handwritten thoughts to keep us encouraged.

My parents always taught me that people don't have to care about you or do anything for you. If they did, that was a bonus and be grateful. Never did I imagine that: 1. I would be out and away from my team, and that 2. the workplace, where business needs can often supersede human needs, would be such a source of comfort and support.

I wasn't the only one who experienced this though. Other team members shared gratitude for the support they and their families received before, during and after their leaves. Comments included feeling like they could not do this anywhere else — stepping out of critical projects and exploring options to reintegrate as the personal situations allowed them to. My colleagues expressed appreciation for the little and big acts of kindness from team members, such as taking time off to help with errands, going to visit them and their loved ones out of town, figuring out ways to share updates more efficiently than text and phone calls, delivering meals, etc.

Oh, and the work — it got done too. That's the thing; this team remained committed to each other, as no one wanted anything to slip through the cracks or for a team member to return to a mess. They took initiative to work with what they had in order to meet customer expectations. Not one time did I receive a phone call or email about a crisis or something not being done while I was out. I am a believer that when you take care of culture, performance usually follows. #Blessed

PREPARING THE TEAM FOR THE FUTURE

I wouldn't trade this journey for anything.

I hope this walk inside of leadership and co-creating an inclusive culture has been helpful to you. While it's not always glorious and you may not get everything right on the first try, it can be rewarding if you are willing to be a student and lover of people.

Why is this important? You are a leader, no matter your title, should you chose to step into the role. The work you do impacts others as well as *how* you or your team work with them. You will experience various seasons of leadership — some include:

- Setting up a new team or department;
- Leading or joining a new cross-functional project team;
- Blending existing teams;
- Leading well-established teams; and
- Working through endings, transitions and new beginnings.

What are some things you can do now to prepare your team to lead without your presence? What about preparing the team to go forward during another team member's extended leave? Job transfer? If a team member wrote a review about your team's culture, what would it say?

Remember, culture supersedes strategy every time. It's the behaviors that show up when no one is looking. Culture is the collective *we*. If you wrote a letter about how you are impacting culture, what would it say?

People will sign up to work for us even before the first day of work because of culture. They frequently share their workplace experiences with others. I encourage you to create a space for you and your team to define the culture, lead and positively impact those you work with. It is incumbent upon us to keep working together to give people the development edge they deserve and unlock human potential to do more — for ourselves and for our organizations.

ABOUT THE AUTHOR

Ann Brown
MS HRD, SPHR

Ann Brown is the founder of The Development Edge, which offers human capital consulting in a variety of areas, as well as individual and group coaching for leaders and executives.

As a talent expert with more than 20 years of experience in the financial services industry, Ann has presented at conferences and served on panel discussions around the United States. She brings passion and energy to each presentation, and participants walk away with key takeaways and toolkits that they can implement immediately. She is available to speak on a variety of topics, including culture and inclusion, talent development, Agile practices in learning and development, change management, onboarding, and more.

Throughout her career, Ann has partnered with executives and provided oversight of strategic people planning with the ongoing integration of talent and performance management.

She is a dynamic and diversified Organizational Development professional who combines strategic thinking and business savvy to leverage and optimize human capital. Ann has the ability to connect the dots at the macro and micro level, ask the right questions and help clients arrive at the right answers for themselves.

Ann is a graduate of Indiana Wesleyan University with a degree in Business Management, and Indiana State University, where she received an MS in Human Resource Development with a specialization in curriculum and instructional design. She has also earned the SPHR human resource designation.

Ann lives in Southern Indiana with her husband, Ronald, and two children, Zoi and Terence. She enjoys watching real wrestling matches, traveling and trying new restaurants with family and friends.

Learn more and contact Ann:

Ann.BrownSPHR@Gmail.com

LinkedIn.com/in/annbrownsphrmshrd

Twitter.com/DevelopmentEdge

Facebook.com/TheDevelopmentEdge

812-989-3903

Chapter Four

JENNIFER P. BROWN
AND MARISSA LEVIN

"Shifts Happen! How Leaders Can Maximize These Opportunities to Create Thriving Cultures"

DEFINING CORPORATE CULTURE: THE SIX MAIN TRIGGERS FOR CULTURE SHIFTS

Leaders change, companies merge, divisions spin off, customer expectations evolve, companies go global and markets transform. These cultural shifts happen every day in organizations. How do you respond? Do you let these shifts tank your organization *or* do you up your game and ensure your organization stays relevant?

To survive a shift and come out thriving, you must first ensure you have a strong culture. Corporate culture is the DNA of every organization. It represents the values, beliefs and behaviors that determine how employees interact inside and outside of the company. It's often explained as a "vibe" or a "feeling." When you walk into a government agency, you'll have a feeling that is quite different from the feeling you'll have when you walk into a technology startup. That feeling is driven by the culture.

There are six components of all corporate cultures that are important to recognize when facing a cultural shift:

1. **Core Values.** What does the company stand for? What is its moral compass? What matters to the company more than profits? Core values are the foundation of every culture.

2. **Vision and Mission.** Where is the company going? Why does it exist? In a strong culture, all employees are aligned to the company direction, and can clearly connect their individual purpose to the larger shared purpose.

3. **The Story.** What is the history of the company? Where did it come from and how did it arrive where it is? Unique or extraordinary events about the company's founding and track record along with key milestones contribute to the story.

4. **The People.** Who are the people that make up your company? What do they stand for? The people are the soul of the company. They align with the values, mission and vision, and fortify the culture every day with their behaviors, decisions and actions.

5. **Rituals and Practices.** What do you and your employees celebrate? How do you thank your employees? Large and small gestures reinforce the cultural promises of a company. Whether it's a company Halloween party or an employee recognition event, rituals back up the values.

6. **The Environment.** Do you have remote employees? Do employees work in offices or cubicles or shared space? As the saying goes, "your vibe attracts your tribe." Your organization configuration dictates how your people will work together.

These six components drive the culture of a company. However, while CEOs clearly value culture, they often struggle to build it. The Korn

Ferry Institute found that 72% of CEOs know culture is important, but only 32% believe their culture is aligned well with their business strategy.[1]

And once you have your culture developed, it can change. The Korn Ferry Institute has identified six primary reasons why cultures experience considerable shifts:[2]

1. **New Leadership.** CEOs step in to implement new strategies or drive a significant transformation. Often, they are responsible for turning around underperforming companies, which will always result in significant cultural disruptions because every aspect of the company will be subject to scrutiny.

2. **Mergers and Acquisitions.** Thirty percent of mergers fail because of simple culture incompatibility.[3] While a merger may look viable on paper, quite often the actual transaction creates tremendous upheaval and an initial financial loss. Integrating two (or more) fully independent entities and streamlining people, processes and products/services creates tremendous chaos because employees cling to what they know.

3. **Spin-Offs.** Companies that choose to divide their organizations into separate entities face challenging culture changes. The new spin-off is essentially a start-up, but its employees are accustomed to a more established, stable culture.

4. **Market, Regulatory and Political Shifts.** External influences can turn a culture on its head. Think Uber, Airbnb, SpaceX and Netflix.

---

1   Korn Ferry. 2014. Korn Ferry Executive Survey, Los Angeles: Korn Ferry.

2   Korn Ferry Institute, *Real World Leadership Report, Part III*, "Creating an Engaging Culture for Greater Impact," 2015.

3   http://www.globoforce.com/gfblog/2012/6-big-mergers-that-were-killed-by-culture/

All of these organizations disrupted and even dismantled seemingly stable industries. For companies that serve the government, the present Administration always drives spending priorities, often forcing companies to adjust their "go-to-market" strategies. These changes create cultural upheaval.

5. **Technology Advancement.** All companies today are swimming against the tide of obsolescence due to rapidly advancing technology. It changes the way business is transacted, it accelerates the pace of business, it demands different skillsets, and it potentially reduces headcount.

6. **Globalization.** All companies are global today. All engage with cultures around the world, transact business using multiple currencies, work in different time zones, and face global competition. For global strategies, cultural evolutions are essential.

THE COST OF CHANGE

These six shifts we've just explored cause change, and change is very hard for people. Research has pinpointed the indirect costs of "organizational trauma" to employees, which are as follows.

Communication breaks down. In times of change, rumors overshadow official communication, resulting in high anxiety levels among employees.

Trust erodes. High stress leads to a self-preservation mindset among employees; they stay focused on themselves and not on their work. Job stress, in the form of absenteeism, healthcare costs and productivity loss, costs US companies approximately $300 billion a year.

Employees feel powerless. Most employees don't have a voice in major decisions that impact them. Consequently, they feel unempowered or victimized.

Employees feel trapped. Downsizing and instability trigger high voluntary turnover. Employees who remain may feel trapped; they often exhibit "survivor" guilt.

Increased unwanted responsibility. Remaining employees are often assigned additional responsibilities of someone who was let go, which can be emotionally challenging.

Grief for what no longer exists. Organizational upheaval is very emotional. Loss of security, loss of feeling of control or competence, loss of relationships, loss of culture, loss of sense of mission/meaning, and feelings of survivor guilt all profoundly impact an employee's psychological state.[4]

A BLUEPRINT FOR HANDLING SHIFTS

When you are hit with a shift, you must ask yourself a series of questions: What is the impact of the shift on my organization's mission, vision, values and behaviors? Its communication strategies? Its talent? Our human resources processes and strategies?

If your company doesn't have well-written and articulated mission, vision and values statements, now's the time to get them in place! If you *do* have them, then you need to review them ASAP to ensure they drive the shift. Otherwise, the shift will drive you, and when that happens, companies fail. Equally important is that you define the employee behaviors supporting your values and objectives. Employees need to understand what defines a "successful employee" in your work environment. Without defining these behaviors, employees will be flying in the dark; and to really make the behaviors stick, involve your employees in defining them.

---

4   http://www.globoforce.com/gfblog/2012/6-big-mergers-that-were-killed-by-culture/

Remember, if people are part of generating, developing or building something, they are much more likely to not only support it, but live it!

If your company doesn't have well-written and articulated mission, vision and values statements, now's the time to get them in place!

The volume on employee communication must be turned up to "high" during a shift. Shifts introduce fear for employees. Their minds go to WIIFM: "What's in it for me?" Without information, employees will make assumptions and imagine unrealistic, worst-case scenarios. This results in lost productivity, increased turn-over and morale issues.

Consequently, you need to not only communicate with employees regularly, but also build trust. Use different communication approaches, such as all-hands meetings, monthly emails from the CEO and/or other management leaders, employee Q&A lunches with management, and demos of new products. Pay special attention to the employees who came over from an acquired company. Remember, they don't know you or your organization; they are starting from a place of distrust.

Above all else, take the time to build and strengthen relationships with all employees. Be present for all employees, have an open-door approach and candidly answer their questions. Managers are the lynchpin in helping employees to understand the changes going on and how they fit in, so be sure you are equipping your managers with key information and messages to share with their employees. In addition, developing a communication plan is critical and should include opportunities for two-way communication — employees need to feel heard. Establishing anonymous surveys to elicit employee questions and feedback are a great way to get employee insights throughout a shift.

Shifts often lead to the need for different types of talent. Remember, the talent that got you where you are today, may not get you to the next level of your business. Shifts often introduce new customers, technology, markets and values, leading to a need for new employee skills, knowledge and behaviors. When you go through a shift, it will be critical to assess your current talent and identify the gaps. Do you need to hire additional talent, train and develop current employees, and/or transition employees out of your organization? Often, all three of these strategies are necessary.

Your HR processes and strategies must live and breathe the values and behaviors you are trying to cultivate. When shifting, review your recruiting and hiring strategies; your new hire orientation program; your performance management and succession planning processes; your learning and development curriculum; and your rewards and recognition programs to ensure they support any cultural changes and new strategic objectives resulting from the shift. For example, you need to ensure that your organization's job postings reflect your company's values and desired behaviors; that values-based interview questions are used; that your orientation communicates the mission, vision, values and behaviors; and that performance plans assess the desired behaviors.

SHIFTS IN ACTION

Let's take a moment to examine three case studies of organizations experiencing major "shifts" — all of which needed a strong partner and a smart plan for navigating the changes and challenges before them.

Case Study #1: An Integration of Two Cultures

A highly-successful company acquired a distressed company. This acquisition resulted in the "new" company having employees in multiple states and countries. There were many differences in these two companies, including HR practices, markets served and leadership philosophies. The CEO quickly saw the issues and brought us in to help.

Our firm, Successful Culture International (SCI), implemented an approach to address the critical aspects of the shift within their culture. We started by helping them develop the mission, vision, values and behaviors reflective of this "new" company. At the same time, we did a needs assessment with employees to assess their concerns. Not surprisingly, a perceived lack of communication was the top issue.

From there, we worked with the leadership team to establish a year-long communication plan that adopted multiple communication channels. In addition, the organization had doubled in size, shining a light on management and leadership. Neither organization's management had ever been provided with training. So, we started by working with leadership to identify the needed management competencies and then implemented a full-scale management university to address critical management gaps. In conjunction with this training, we provided one-on-one coaching to the senior leaders.

We also worked with the organization to strengthen its HR processes in support of its culture. For example, values-based interview questions were developed and included in the interview process along with updated job descriptions that focused on behaviors needed to support the culture and objectives. In addition, a new and improved company overview was added to the orientation, new compensation plans were established, and a recognition program by which employees could recognize their peers and management was introduced.

Case Study #2: An Industry Roll-Up of Several Small Businesses

A private equity firm funded the roll-up of multiple small businesses (all less than $10 million) and appointed a CEO to lead the newly created firm. The founders of the acquired firms have always led their own firms, each with their own distinctive cultures. The new CEO's objective was to create a single umbrella culture that unified the founders and their employees, and that gave them a single core value system, mission and vision to follow. The ultimate purpose of the roll-up was to create a single entity to be acquired by one of the industry giants, so healthy financial performance across all businesses was critical.

SCI applied its proven model to establish an overarching culture and unify all disparate businesses:

- The CEO chose to start from scratch to create a new set of core values, a mission statement and a vision statement. To ensure buy-in, we included all founders in the process. We sent out surveys for all three of the foundational elements, and then worked through our proprietary process to create the statements.

- We facilitated an offsite retreat to educate the leadership team on the connection between culture and leadership, and rolled out the new identity elements, which included the vision, mission, values, and desired employee behaviors.

- We trained the founders how to take the new information back to their employees.

- We instituted a strong, proactive company-wide communications strategy to reinforce the values, mission and vision, and to continue knocking down the silos between the individual businesses.

- Concurrently, we launched an anonymous organizational assessment with the leadership team and their direct reports to get candid feedback about what was and was not working.

- We implemented one-on-one coaching with all the founders to work on what was holding them back from being fully engaged, and to thoroughly understand their personal motivations for staying with the company. Some were motivated by money, others were not. Some were motivated by meaning and purpose. Others had difficulty letting go.

- Because the company has ambitious growth plans and hiring needs, we re-engineered their recruiting, hiring and onboarding process to be values-based and culture-centric. This will ensure that all future hires align to the overarching culture.

💼 Case Study #3: Industry Disruptor

A disruptive firm in the medical industry invested millions of dollars developing its platform over the first three years of the company's life. They focused only on the technology. When the time came to launch, they wanted to attract the very best developers and leaders in a highly competitive space who would be committed to the company for the long haul. They also wanted to be known for a standout culture.

SCI applied its proven model to define and strengthen the company culture and to establish a culture-centric recruiting and onboarding process. We achieved this in many ways.

First, we used our processes to define the company's values, mission and vision. We rolled these out to the entire company, and educated the company on the connection between culture, values and leadership.

We then led employees through an exercise of "shared responsibility," in which they collectively defined the desired and expected behaviors for each value, and then committed to living them.

We also led the company's recruiting process alongside their COO to ensure the company hired for both technical and cultural fit. We wrote the job descriptions, formulated the interview questions, attended job fairs, conducted interviews and made recommendations. We formally onboarded all new employees in satellite offices.

**Repairing, building and maintaining
a healthy culture that aligns to business strategy
takes intentional and ongoing effort.**

CULTURE IS A CONTINUOUS PROCESS

As our case studies demonstrate, repairing, building and maintaining a healthy culture that aligns to business strategy takes intentional and ongoing effort. Just as you get done conquering one shift, another shift will be coming your way. Therefore, you can never take your eye off your culture.

- Do you have a well-articulated mission, vision and values that are aligned with your business strategy?

- Is the right talent in place to achieve your business objectives?

- Are your HR processes running seamlessly and in support of your goals?

- Are you communicating continuously to your employees?

Shifts happen: Don't let them scare you. No matter which shifts are going on in your organization, there are always distinct opportunities to maximize these moments to create a thriving culture that drives growth in a sustainable, differentiated way. Not sure how to get started? We'd love to help you. Give us a call.

ABOUT THE AUTHORS

Jennifer P. Brown
MBA, SPHR, SHRM-SCP

Jennifer "Jen" Brown's love of organizational development and human resources started when she interned during her sophomore year in college with the Association for Training and Development. Today she is co-founder and Managing Partner of Successful Culture International and founder and CEO of PeopleTactics LLC.

Having led major corporate functions and advised executives during steady and turbulent times, Jen has extensive first-hand experience in driving organizational change at a strategic level and facilitating rapid personal improvement in individuals. She has worked in diverse environments, including financial, banking, government contracting manufacturing, professional services, consumer goods, real estate, insurance, nonprofits, legal, hospitality, retail, transportation and utilities.

Jen is a business-focused Human Resources and Organizational Effectiveness leader who knows that a business is only as strong as its people. Her goal in working with clients is to provide thoughtful, specialized and appropriate business solutions to challenging HR, Leadership and Organizational Development issues.

She spent the first part of her career in Andersen Consulting's (Accenture) Change Management practice and then held various senior roles at Freddie Mac to include Manager, Training and Development; Director, HR Business Partner; Director of Recruiting; and Director of HR Business Operations. For the past 15 years, she has been providing HR and organizational development consulting and advisory services focused on:

- Strategy and organizational development steeped in a company's vision, mission, values and desired employee behaviors;

- Executive and management leadership development and coaching;

- Employee training and development;

- Employee attraction and engagement;

- Performance management; and

- HR strategy development, function establishment and turn-around situations.

Jennifer is a frequent speaker on HR and Organizational Development topics and has been featured in the Washington Business Report (WJLA-TV), *U.S. News & World Report*, Business News Daily, monster. com, recuiter.com, and SMART CEO. Jennifer has been an adjunct faculty member with the Robert H. Smith School of Business at the University of Maryland, where she taught several HR courses at the undergraduate and graduate level. She earned a Master of Business Administration (specialized in HR and Organizational Development) and Bachelor of Science (major in Personnel/Labor Relations) from the University of Maryland. Jennifer is also certified as a Senior Professional in Human Resources (SPHR and SHRM-SCP).

Jen lives in Northern Virginia with her husband and yellow lab. Her two children are in college and she loves Jazzercise!

Learn more and contact Jen:

Jen@successfulculture.com

Jen@peopletactics.com

SuccessfulCultureInternational.com

SuccessfulCulture.com

PeopleTactics.com

LinkedIn.com/in/jenbrownhr

Twitter.com/jenpbrownhr

Facebook.com/SuccessfulCultureInternational

Marissa Levin

MA, HRD & OD

A 25-year entrepreneur, speaker, & globally recognized growth strategist, Marissa Levin's lifetime legacy mission is to educate, equip, and empower 100 million entrepreneurs and leaders with the skillsets and mindsets they need to reach their greatest potential.

Marissa's entrepreneurial journey began in 1995 when she launched Information Experts, a strategic communications and education firm. She launched her firm as a solopreneur with a $35,000 contract and led/grew the organization to approximately $15 million in revenue until she departed the thriving organization to build her next enterprise.

Under her leadership, Information Experts won more than 80 awards for creativity and leadership, was named to the *Inc. 5000* List of America's Fastest Growing Companies for 2009, 2010, and 2011, won the 2010 SmartCEO GovStar Industry Star Award, and was known as a trailblazer in establishing an extraordinary employee-centric culture that fully supported work-life integration and a core value of "responsible flexibility."

In 2012, she launched Successful Culture, a leadership consulting organization that helps CEOs master the three most critical aspects of business growth: leadership development, strategy formulation and execution, and organizational culture assessment and improvement.

In 2017, she co-founded Women's CEO Roundtable, a professionally facilitated year-long program for women business owners from noncompeting organizations that are committed to scaling beyond $1 million in revenue.

Also in 2017, Marissa merged Successful Culture with PeopleTactics, a national leader in Strategic HR Consulting to launch Successful Culture International (SCI), a global corporate culture consultancy that leads organizations undergoing significant transformation through a proven model to define, stabilize, and strengthen organizational cultures. SCI also works with emerging companies to help define their corporate cultures so that they can attract, hire and retain the best talent.

Marissa is also the regional Chair for Women Presidents Organization, an international community of multi-million-dollar women business owners, for whom she facilitates monthly CEO roundtables.

Marissa is the author of the #1 best-selling book *Built to SCALE: How Top Companies Create Breakthrough Growth Through Exceptional Advisory Boards*. Using Marissa's patented SCALE Model, SCI helps CEOs select and implement highly effective advisory boards, which is an essential strategy for any business looking to grow exponentially.

Finally, Marissa is a leadership columnist for *Inc. Magazine.*

Marissa holds a Master's Degree in Human Resources Development & Organizational Development, is a credentialed coach certified by International Coach Federation (ICF), is certified in Instructional Systems Design, and is a Certified Mastermind Facilitator.

Marissa lives in Northern Virginia with her husband Adam, and her Golden Doodle Lexie. She is the mother of two sons, ages 18 and 21. Marissa loves to write and read, and enjoys live music and theatre.

Learn more and contact Marissa:

Marissa@SuccessfulCulture.com

SuccessfulCultureInternational.com

SuccessfulCulture.com

LinkedIn.com/in/MarissaLevin1

Twitter.com/MarissaLevin

Instagram.com/MarissaLevin1

Facebook.com/SuccessfulCultureInternational

ABOUT THE COLLABORATION BETWEEN CO-AUTHORS JEN AND MARISSA

In 2017, Marissa and Jen combined forces to launch Successful Culture International (SCI). They have been close friends and business associates for 15 years. Throughout this period, they've collaborated on dozens of initiatives and have more than 50 years of experience helping organizations build their most engaging, productive cultures; implement supporting human resources strategies; and develop transformational leaders and teams. They share a passion for building positive, extraordinary environments where employees love to work and contribute to their organization's success.

SCI is a global corporate culture consultancy that leads organizations undergoing significant transformation through a proven model to define, stabilize and strengthen organizational cultures. SCI also works with emerging companies to help define their corporate cultures so that they can attract, hire and retain the best talent.

Chapter Five

WENDI E. ELDH

"Be Your Own Performance Manager"

Here's the deal: In almost every other facet of our lives, we take charge. For example, if you plan to buy a new house, what do you do? You research neighborhoods, housing prices, interest rates and school districts. Would you ever ask your real estate agent just to tell you where to live and which house to buy? Would you ever skip all that vital research and homework? Probably not.

But each year at our jobs, many of us receive our performance goals and measures, work hard, and then passively sit back and wait for the rating verdict. Does this make sense? *Of course not!*

Shouldn't we take a more active role in managing our performance and advocating for ourselves? The truth is that you are more than a cog in a wheel — and more than just the personal brand you've been encouraged to cultivate. You are the brand manager, the keeper of the keys, the master of your universe … you get the idea.

If you aren't being an active participant in the performance management process, then there's a strong chance you're a passive recipient instead.

In my workshop, "Be Your Own Performance Manager," attendees learn a process and multiple strategies for proactively taking part in their organization's performance management system, allowing them to maximize their potential and create workplace engagement.

In this chapter, we will drill down and look at two essential strategies for bolstering your advocacy role: tracking and writing about your performance.

WHY DO WE STRUGGLE TO WRITE ABOUT OURSELVES?

If you're like most working people, and you struggle to capture and tell the story of your impact, skills and value to your organization, read on. Here you will consider why you should share your successes, how to track your performance all year, and how to write powerful accomplishments.

Why are we able to sing the praises of others, but undersell ourselves?

I recently read an accomplishment report that offered these successes: "I timely attended all required training," and "I helped work on a process." Pretty underwhelming descriptions, right?

This Federal government employee, whom we'll call Michelle, good-naturedly accepted my feedback that she'd done little to shed light on her impact — and she'd made plenty. For example, her process work involved leading a team of experts from four organizations to create a more seamless process. It worked, and she saved her organization (and her team) time, money and undue headaches, in addition to building stronger alliances with the other organizations. These actions made a significant difference, yet she did little to share the impact with her boss.

Why? Michelle assumed her boss already knew, and she didn't want to brag. Plus, she felt it wasn't a big deal. Only in answering my questions — "Why did you want to change the process?" and "What was the outcome?" — was Michelle able to see and appreciate the true impact of her work.

Why are we able to sing the praises of others, but undersell ourselves?

Our reasons for shortchanging our descriptions of our work can include:

- Being too busy to do the reflection and writing

- Believing that leadership is just going through the motions of asking or won't care

- Not wanting to draw attention to ourselves

- Thinking that our actions should speak for themselves.

When we do good work but share minimal details about it, we are leaving a lot on the table — lost opportunities to show our value, cultivate our talent, create opportunities and maintain our workplace engagement.

Steuart Henderson Britt, renowned marketing and consumer psychologist, famously said: "Doing business without advertising is like winking at someone in the dark. You know what you are doing but nobody else does." (Okay, he actually said winking at "a girl," but let's note that he said this a LONG time ago.)

We need to stop winking in the dark and instead take a robust role in this process.

WHY SHOULD I SHARPEN THESE SKILLS?

At first glance, the answer seems obvious: You should be your own best advocate. But the benefits extend beyond what you might initially conceive. They can include the following:

Self-Reflection: When you track your performance closely and regularly, you see how you spend your time, which projects get your pulse racing and where you've demonstrated mastery. Looking inward allows you to identify your strengths, preferences and skill gaps.

Expanded Focus: Coordinating your efforts with leadership, gaining clarity on goals and performance measures, and keeping apprised of shifting priorities all tend to expand your focus from myopic to wide-ranging.

Engagement: Workplace engagement means we are plugged in — excited to go to work, not dreading it. Honestly self-reflecting and maintaining alignment help you become — and stay — engaged.

Transportability: These are transferable skills that can enable you to write more impactful resumes and staff performance reports, give better interviews, submit more competitive applications and develop a clearer self-brand.

OKAY, I'M CONVINCED, BUT NOW WHAT? (AKA, HOW DO I TRACK AND WRITE ABOUT MY PERFORMANCE?)

Tracking Your Performance

Performance Tracking Quiz

Yes   No

☐ ☐ Have you recently (or ever) had a month-long headache because of a workplace problem?

☐ ☐ Have you ever wrapped up a project and sighed with relief that it was FINALLY over?

☐ ☐ Have you ever navigated a difficult interaction with an individual or a group?

If you answered "yes" to any of these questions, you probably have an accomplishment that's worth writing about. Your boss likely knows as well as you do that the most important outcomes are often in the messiest work and the least glamorous roles, so be sure to capture these experiences and then share them.

The most important outcomes are often in the messiest work and the least glamorous roles.

Prompting Questions

Take a moment to contemplate your answers to the following questions:

- How am I spending my time?
- Have I taken on special projects?
- Have I sought to solve problems?
- What special skills do I have?
- How am I differentiated from my colleagues?
- Have I done things not in my job description and by my own initiative?

What Goes on the Highlight Reel?

Performance criteria are usually correlated to measurable outcomes — how much money, time or effort we saved; how many people we managed; the number of projects we completed on or before deadline; and so on. And while you should capture this vital information, don't overlook contributions in other important categories:

Leading People

Being Aware of the Big Picture

Tolerating Ambiguity

Organizing and Planning

Using Analytical or Creative Problem Solving Skills

Effectively Making Decisions

Maintaining a Team Focus

Adhering to Policies and Procedures

Being Versatile

Being Responsive

Having Emotional Intelligence and Interpersonal Skills

Using Peacemaking Skills

Let's consider a couple of examples …

Suppose your organization is experiencing deep change; in fact, your position and office could well be on the chopping block. Gossip is rampant, and people are stressed and unfocused. Yet you maintain a sense of equanimity, outperforming your goals while also being aware of shifting priorities. In this instance, writing only about outperforming your goals would undersell the fact that you're doing this within the context of upheaval and ambiguity.

Or suppose your office caters to external clients who frequently make last-minute requests. Though everyone on your team handles these requests, you seem to get at least 15% more calls than your peers. Why? Your manager tells you that clients view you as the most responsive. While the fact that you serve the most clients is important, the rationale behind it — your responsiveness — is equally so.

Tracking It Year-Round

When we first complete a project, solve a problem or exceed expectations in some manner, it feels significant and we don't expect to forget it. But when we sit down to write about our accomplishments, we may forget tasks entirely or remember only the basic outline, and thus not include how we overcame roadblocks or created work-arounds.

Tracking performance doesn't need to be complex or time consuming.

For example, during a recent workshop, one attendee, Bill, struggled to think of an accomplishment. He told me, "The main thing is that I tend to come in on the weekend if I need to." I asked him to explain why he might need to do this. "Well, the last time was because I needed to submit some important paperwork that no one else had taken care of." We explored this a bit and he related that if he had not submitted the paperwork, his office would have missed a deadline, resulting in serious repercussions. Although it wasn't his job to file the paperwork, he knew it was imperative. By not tracking his performance, Bill not only forgot about this act, but also lost its significance. This alone was a notable accomplishment, and it was heightened when tied to a pattern of responsibly handling extra work and deadlines.

Tracking performance doesn't need to be complex or time consuming. It can be as simple as keeping a folder (paper or electronic) handy for jotting notes in real time. The key is to create a system you'll use and to sketch out the details so that when it comes to writing, you'll remember the details that make your accomplishments worth mentioning.

WRITING ABOUT YOUR PERFORMANCE

An effectively written accomplishment tells the compelling story of a situation: a challenge within that situation, how you handled that challenge, and the important results from your action. In Bill's case, he knew his office was required to file annual paperwork to maintain programmatic compliance; he discovered his office would miss the deadline if he didn't act; he filed the needed paperwork; and he saved his organization from serious repercussions.

While models vary for describing performance, most will ask you to include the **C**ontext that existed, the **C**hallenge you faced, the **A**ction you took, and the **R**esult (CCAR). If a mnemonic device helps, consider using SOAR (Situation, Obstacle, Action, and Result).

CCAR		**SOAR**
Context that existed		**S**ituation
Challenge you faced	**OR**	**O**bstacle
Action you took		**A**ction
Result		**R**esult

Here are other important writing tips:

✓ Don't just list your work activities. The fact that you have written reports, crafted budgets, attended meetings or training, submitted invoices, and essentially done your job is not remarkable. What you are after is the *result* of that activity: "I researched and wrote a market report (an activity) that was the impetus for a new product line rolled out last year that is already profitable (result)." (Note that the CCAR model would shed light on the situation that led you to do this research, note any challenges you faced, highlight your research and report, and further discuss the benefits to your organization.)

✓ Focus on a few important accomplishments that represent your overall performance and be sure to link these to organizational goals and priorities when you can.

✓ Provide enough context for the reader to understand the circumstances but don't go into needless detail. Keep it crisp and on point.

✓ Maintain objectivity by avoiding flowery language and absolutes. Example: "I am always the very best team leader in our organization" versus "When I was promoted to lead the development team, productivity was down, and climate culture surveys indicated that staff were disengaged and frustrated by the rapid changes that had taken place during the past five years. I set several goals, primarily focusing on improving morale and increasing productivity. I have spent the past 12 months seeking to transform the culture of my team, using team- and trust-building techniques and collaborative tools. By year's end, our team productivity had increased by 20%, employee absences had decreased by 30% and staff have reported a better sense of purpose." Note that this accomplishment would likely be longer than what I have here because it would describe the context and the team leader's actions in more detail. When it comes to demonstrating your value to your organization, the details matter.

✓ Prefer the active voice: Use "I" to identify clearly that the action taken was yours and use meaningful verbs when you can.

✓ If using bullet points, maintain parallel structure.

✓ Identify colleagues or staff in your accomplishment only if the reference is positive or neutral — no tossing anyone under the bus.

✓ When possible, tie the accomplishment to your overall performance, to a specific performance goal, and to overarching organizational goals — and take the result as far out as is reasonable. In Bill's case, it wasn't just his going to work on a Saturday — it was handling this task for another staff member, protecting his leadership from the negative repercussions and ensuring the organization remained compliant.

✓ Use linking words to guide the reader through your narrative. For example, you might write "I was faced with …" and then have words such as "Therefore, I decided to …" followed at last by something such as, "Ultimately," "In the end" or "The result was …"

Let's look back at Michelle's situation through the lens of CCAR. You'll recall that Michelle was the government employee who led a collaboration of four departments through the creation of an important new process, but didn't know how to talk about it and take credit for the gravity of this work. With the CCAR framework, Michelle is able to write about this achievement in a powerful way:

"Our office handles requests for reasonable accommodations equipment. We work with three organizations to handle the procurement, shipping and placement of this equipment, which can range from special chairs and keyboards to screen reading software with synthesized speech capabilities. I noticed that the existing process for ordering and receiving new equipment duplicated effort and was needlessly slow. I began looking for opportunities to streamline the process without affecting our compliance with existing rules and directives. Over five months, I shepherded a process change by troubleshooting the situation, engaging with each organization, proposing multiple solutions and getting buy-in from all involved parties. After seeking approval from my leadership, I was able to institute my proposed changes. Ultimately, my changes have cut average processing time by more than half, from 15 days to 7 days. In our office alone, we are saving approximately 48 staff hours a week, and we have received excellent feedback from our clients about our responsiveness to their requests."

YOUR TURN

Why don't you give it a try? Think of an accomplishment from the past three to six months — one that was especially challenging. (Remember: Headaches and messes often yield notable accomplishments.) Sketch out the context, the challenge, the action you took to manage that challenge and the result.

Context:

_____

_____

Challenge:

_____

_____

Action:

_____

_____

Result:

_____

_____

Then pull these elements into a paragraph (or several) that tells the story in a compelling manner. Review the list of writing tips and make edits as needed.

_____

_____

_____

_____

_____

_____

_____

_____

Good job!

PUTTING IT ALL TOGETHER (A RECAP AND A CHECKLIST)

Let's now recap how you should track and write skillfully about your performance:

Be your own advocate.

Honestly reflect on your strengths, preferences, development opportunities and skill gaps as you take on this advocacy role.

Track your performance and reap the many benefits of doing so, including increased workplace engagement.

Write powerful accomplishments to convey your value to the organization and to bolster your competence at writing resumes, giving amazing interviews and more.

Don't "wink in the dark."

Checklist

- ✓ Keep at your fingertips a copy of your current work goals and performance measures.

- ✓ Create a simple tracking system — which can be as low-tech as a manila folder — where you can make note of your accomplishments.

- ✓ Print or save copies of emails or letters of kudos and add these to your tracking system.

- ✓ Put a bi-weekly or monthly reminder on your calendar to be sure you have captured important tasks, outcomes or roles.

- ✓ Seek out feedback from your boss and colleagues about what you have done well and where you can be doing things differently.

- ✓ Communicate with your leadership to understand current priorities.

- ✓ Don't wait until the last minute to begin writing about yourself. *Write*. Let the writing cool a bit. Revisit and edit. Repeat until you are satisfied that you have fully captured your hard work and successes.

When it comes to writing about your accomplishments and preparing for a truly outstanding performance review in which you get fully recognized for all you've achieved, there's no time like the present. You're doing the work *now* and making a difference *now*.

Be sure to capture the details and the significance *now*. They say that the best time to plant a tree is today, and I can't help but think that your success, satisfaction and longevity at your current job is a lot like that tree. It's time to be your own performance manager. You can do this!

ABOUT THE AUTHOR

Wendi E. Eldh

For more than 24 years, Wendi Eldh has been helping organizations achieve better results and enhanced communication through customized training and targeted coaching as founder of Eldh & Associates. A trainer, curriculum designer, course facilitator, coach and consultant, Wendi serves both the public and private sectors. Her clients include the USDA, FDIC, SEC, CMS, BAE Systems, Department of Defense, U.S. Navy and many more.

Wendi brings wit, humor and the right dose of challenge to the classroom, delivering customized, interactive workshops on dozens of topics, including executive communication, performance management, influence and interpersonal communication. Wendi believes workplace engagement is the responsibility of both managers and staff, and she has developed performance management workshops for both audiences. Her customized writing workshops cover a range of writing styles, such as email, directives, policy guidance, reports, audits and accomplishments.

Before launching her business, Wendi was a journalist. Her 10-year media career included positions as a sports writer, weather reporter, disc jockey, radio news reporter, TV news reporter for a CNN affiliate, Gannett daily newspaper reporter and editor for a U.S. military magazine in Europe. She was also the Internal Communications Manager for Merchants National Bank in Germany.

Wendi holds a BS in Journalism with a broadcast emphasis from San Diego State University and a Master's in Education in Human Resources Development, with an emphasis on curriculum design and delivery to adult learners, from Boston University.

Wendi fosters dogs, loves music and dancing, must have good coffee and chocolate, and has a quirky sense of humor. She is afraid of roller coasters.

Wendi would love to hear about your accomplishments. You can share them or learn more about her workshops at www.GetExcellentTraining.com or www.WendiEldh.com.

Learn more and contact Wendi:

WendiEldh@GetExcellentTraining.com

WendiEldh@Verizon.net

LinkedIn.com/in/wendi-eldh-55980bb

703-799-6543

703-674-8861

Chapter Six

MS. RANDI FRANK

"Recruiting the Right Talent for Your Organization"

If you want to unlock human potential at the workplace, you need to have the right team working *for* you and *with* you. To do this, you need to recruit the correct candidates for your unique organization and not just "hire employees." It's all about fit.

Hiring employees is a process of advertising the position, and praying the right person applies and is interviewed. Recruiting for candidates, on the other hand, means first understanding your organization, the position, the culture and the desired skills and personality of the best person who fits your team.

It's vital to understand how to recruit and attract new employees who meet your needs, because the only way to unlock human potential in the workplace is to first welcome the right people into the organization. Based on my experience having conducted more than 50 executive searches in the past, I suggest the following nine key steps to hiring the right candidates. This method can be used for both executive and non-executive positions.

So where do you start?

First, review all materials on the position. Develop or revise the job description to meet the real need. The best time to review a position is when you have a vacancy. If there's an existing job description, make sure it is accurate for the position today and for the current needs of the organization. This is a perfect time to decide whether the position is still the right fit for the organization or whether it's time to change the position to meet the new, evolving and/or expanding needs of the workplace.

Talk with the other members of the department and management staff to make sure you know what is needed for this vacant position. Then, develop or revise a job description to reflect the changes to include:

- Appropriate equipment used
- Education and experience needed
- Skills, knowledge and abilities required
- Responsibilities and objectives of the position.

Look at what work was assigned to and completed by the previous employee. Is that what the organization still needs today? Is it time to increase the responsibilities of the position to a supervisor or management level? Do you need more technical experience for this position to meet the needs of your customers/clients? What were some of the complaints from the department in the past that might indicate you need different skills and resources the next time around? If you make a change in the position, make sure you research the salary and determine whether you have enough funds in the budget for the change.

Second, develop a profile of the position to mail and email to potential candidates. Why is this important? Because recruiting for talent means appealing to the right people. It's imperative that you make your position stand out among all the other advertisements. A well-written profile tells candidates that you have really thought about the position and the type of candidates you want to attract to your organization. The profile can be put into many formats, depending upon the specific needs and type of media you use. It can be a colorful PDF attached to an email, or a color brochure that is mailed or shared at meetings and job fairs. You can also refer to the profile in your advertisement, providing a web address where candidates can learn more. That way, you spend less on the advertisement and more on the development of the profile.

Recruiting for candidates means first understanding your organization, the position, the culture, and the desired skills and personality of the best person who fits your team.

A great profile will enable candidates to really get to know your organization. It should use colorful pictures and catchy phrases to capture readers' attention so they want to read more about the position, your organization and why they should be interested in your exciting opportunity.

As a recruitment and executive search expert, I typically spend two to three days with a client really getting to know their organization and the position so I can prepare an effective profile. I meet with all the relevant stakeholders. For entry-level positions, you may need to plan for less time to develop a shorter profile.

The job profile should sell the position and your company or agency through pictures and detailed information to attract professional, enthusiastic candidates. Once a profile is developed, it can be used again and again with slight changes for different types of positions. The profile will let candidates know what is expected and answer many of their questions;

it can also serve to screen candidates who don't have the qualifications and experience to handle the position as described.

The profile should include, at the minimum:

- Description of the organization and/or department
- Financial information about the organization
- Job description, job qualifications, challenges facing the position
- Mission statement, as well as goals and objectives for the organization as a whole and for the department or business unit that is hiring
- Positive, notable programs or accomplishments
- Ideal and personal characteristics needed for the candidate (e.g. detail oriented, proactive, etc.)
- Organizational culture and information about the community if you are advertising nationally and seeking to attract candidates who will be making a move; and
- Management style desired (e.g., team builder, strong budget skills, excellent leadership and communication skill to promote projects, etc.).

A job profile can also be used for entry-level positions by using shorter summaries of the information listed above.

Resources

Samples of position profiles can be found on my website under executive searches at www.RandiFrank.com.

Third, develop a timetable for your recruitment. To develop the timetable for your recruitment, you need to know when you want to fill the position and work backward. Set the date for the new employee to start, and then anticipate the time needed for each step so you know when to start the recruitment.

Unfortunately, you won't always have the luxury of knowing when a position will be vacant, and you may therefore need to establish dates for each step and move forward as quickly as you can to fill the position. Flexibility is key because you can't always anticipate the unexpected, such as candidates needing to give a longer period of notice to their previous employer, a hiring manager's vacation during the interview week, etc.

Your timetable for recruitment should include accommodating and scheduling each of the following steps:

- Evaluating the position and needs of your organization
- Reviewing, developing or revising the job description
- Developing an advertisement and profile about the position
- Placing an advertisement, giving at least two weeks for candidates to respond (and three to four weeks for executives)
- Proactively recruiting through various methods *(see step five below for more details)* in addition to your advertisement
- Screening applications and resumes
- Ranking candidates
- Testing candidates (written, oral or practical examinations, such as telephone interviews or driving tests, customer service testing, technology testing, etc.)
- Interviewing top candidates with appropriate staff and managers
- Conducting final interviews
- Completing background and reference checks

- Preparing a job offer with a date set for your new employee to join your organization.

Fourth, decide on types and amount of advertising to be used. This is always a difficult decision because you want to get the word out to as many candidates as possible, but you don't want to over-extend your budget. I recommend you look at targeting the correct candidates by focusing on publications and websites that relate to the position. For example, if you are looking for a chief financial officer, you might advertise with professional associations that have memberships of finance officers or CPAs. If you are looking for a human resources director for a business, then you might advertise with the Society for Human Resource Management (SHRM) and their various chapters. Advertising in a newspaper for these types of positions will not produce as many qualified candidates compared to advertising with the relevant professional associations.

Another decision that needs to be made is whether to do a national or local search. Entry-level positions lend themselves to local searches, but most professional and management positions should include a national search. You would be surprised by how many people are willing to move away or to come back home or move to be close to family.

Using professional association websites will enable you to reach a local and national audience. One search I conducted tripled the number of applications because we used professional associations instead of local newspapers.

Fifth, develop list of target candidates and professional organizations to tap for qualified candidates. Email, or mail literature to target candidates or call them to share the news. Once you have your profile and advertisement prepared, you are ready to send out the word about your position. In addition to the advertisement, you need to contact professionals in the field and let them know you have a vacant position that is a great opportunity. Ask colleagues to spread the word about your position (let your LinkedIn network know about the vacancy and post on other social media sites). Once you have found the appropriate professional associations, you can email the officers of the group and ask them to spread the word. Always attach your colorful profile to your communications. Many of the professional associations will also email your information to their membership or post your position on their website for free or a low price. Many professional associations also have state chapters, so you can reach out to those officers also. If you have an address list of potential candidates, then mail your profile.

The more people you contact, the better the chance you will find the person who knows the perfect candidate for you.

In other words, through "networking" (online and off-line), you will conduct a professional search for the best-qualified candidates and invite them to apply for the position. The more people you contact, the better the chance you will find the person who knows the perfect candidate for you.

Sixth, receive, review and evaluate candidates' materials. Develop a rating system to help you determine which candidates are most qualified and appear to be a great fit for the position. Once you start receiving resumes for a position, create a list with candidates' first and last names and email addresses (or postal address if no email is provided). This way, you can keep track of the number of candidates and send them a thank you email or note. Once you start reviewing the resumes, you can separate them into piles of "meets minimum requirements" or "does not meet minimum requirements," and record this on your list. Next, review the candidates with minimum requirements and evaluate them based on the job description and needs of the organization to determine your top candidates. Sometimes I need to conduct a short telephone interview of candidates to determine if they meet the minimum requirements — especially with senior executives who don't list all the details in their resumes.

There are many ways to rate candidates: Put them into A, B and C candidate piles or use a number system. For example, if the position requires a Bachelor's degree and prefers a Master's degree, you can give candidates with the Master's degrees more points. If the position requires five years of experience, you can give candidates one point for five years of experience, two points for six to seven years, three points for eight to nine years, and four points for candidates with 10 or more years of experience. You can also rate the type of experience they have as it relates to your position. Is their experience in the same industry? If so, does that mean they will fit in better with your organization? Some companies are looking for diversity of experience, and candidates may receive more points for that type of diverse experience. Candidates with the most points, or the "A" candidates, should then be reviewed in more detail by the hiring manager for further screening.

Seventh, develop a written evaluation form for top candidates to complete. There is a chance that you will have more than 20 top candidates, yet you do not want to interview that many. Using written evaluations or other tests can reduce the number of top candidates called for interviews. Written questionnaires also highlight the candidates' writing style and ability to present information.

Written evaluations can include facts and figures about candidates' backgrounds, such as number of years of experience in specific tasks related to the position. For example, for a human resource director, you may want to

know if they have experience with benefit administration, labor relations, recruitment, performance management and pension administration. Once you have gathered general facts about a person's background,
you can proceed to essay questions related to their field of study. For
example, for a police chief, you may want to know how they handled
implementing community policing programs in their past community, or
how they handled promotions or discipline in the past. For a CFO, you
will want to know the size of budget and number of separate accounts
they managed, and how they managed reduced revenues. I have found
that using these types of written documents separates the best of the best
candidates and identifies the ones you want to interview. Typically, candidates are required to complete their questionnaires within a week. Those
who don't respond at all ultimately send you valuable unspoken feedback
(i.e., they see the questions and realized the position is not for them, or
they suffer from big egos and think they're too good to have to answer).

Eighth, develop an interview process for top candidates. The interview
process can take many formats, depending upon the organization. Panel
interviews can be arranged for candidates to meet various members of
the management team at one time, so they can work together to select
the top candidate. Some panels are also made up of experts in the
field from outside the organization; they serve as a screening panel for
management to create a list of the top three candidates. Some interviews
are one-on-one interviews with the hiring manager or round-robin
scenarios that use one-on-one interviews with various members of the
organization, such as Human Resources, Operations and the CEO.
Interviews can also include a tour of your facility and organization,
where the candidates are introduced to many employees to observe their
people skills. Some interviews entail the candidate making presenta-
tions on their background or topics of interest in the field to test their
skill in public speaking. For example, a University Environmental Safety

Director candidate was asked to present a speech on chemistry laboratory safety procedures.

Once an interview format has been determined, make the arrangements. All participants should receive a calendar of events with names and resumes, times and locations. All candidates should also receive information about the format, who they will be meeting with, and specific locations and logistics, such as parking or hotel arrangements, if necessary.

Ninth, conduct first and second interviews as necessary. Conduct reference/background checks on top candidates as required.
Sometimes one interview is all that is needed because all involved agree on the top candidate. In other situations, a second interview is needed to determine the right fit and to delve deeper into each of the top candidates. As long as you — the employer — are paying for the expenses related to the interview, the candidates will not mind returning for extra interviews because it will enable them to learn more about the organization. Remember, they are interviewing you as much as you are interviewing them. Remember that second interviews should be conducted quickly so you don't lose the best candidates to other employers. Candidates acknowledge that a thorough process is important, but if it drags on then you could tarnish the brand of your organization, which is why an organized, planned recruitment process is critical.

I recommend background and reference checks to ensure there are no surprises in the future. Depending upon the position, you may want to do a drivers' license check, criminal and civil court checks, credit check, education verification, Google check and, of course, reference checks.

Once this is complete to your satisfaction, offer the candidate the position and negotiate a salary, starting date and other arrangements. Be aware that you may need to make a conditional offer before you can conduct a physical for certain positions, such as truck driver, laborer or mechanic in accordance with the Americans with Disability Act. Some organizations also provide a conditional offer while they are conducting the background and reference check work.

Remember, they are interviewing you as much as you are interviewing them.

---

* * *

And there you have it — nine thoughtful steps for recruiting the right talent for your organization. You can follow this guide yourself or use an experienced professional to assist you with the process. Whatever way you choose to go about it, these steps are proven to help lead you to the right candidate for your organization. Most importantly, these activities will greatly improve the likelihood that your new employee is best suited to become part of the team, and to promote your mission and customer services. The greater good — stronger teams, a stronger company and more satisfied customers — begins with each individual you hire. Want to unlock the human potential for a great workplace? Being deliberate and smart about your talent recruitment strategy is the first step in achieving that goal.

ABOUT THE AUTHOR

Ms. Randi Frank
MPA

Randi Frank has more than 30 years of successful experience as a manager and administrator with various organizations in capacities including: Human Resources Manager, Assistant Town Manager, Purchasing Agent, Risk Manager, Budget/Management Analyst, Grants Writer and Administrator.

Randi has a Master's degree in Public Administration from the University of Southern California and a Bachelor's degree in Urban Affairs from the University of Rhode Island. She is a Certified Risk Manager and a Certified School Business Manager.

Randi founded her company, Randi Frank Consulting, LLC, in 2000 and as its President has focused on assisting her clients with Human Resources Consulting Services along with general administrative or management assistance. Her business has been recognized across the nation for its hands-on quality service; her company received Certified Woman Owned Business status in Connecticut, Louisville and Kentucky.

Her clients include small business, public sector agencies and non-profit organizations. Some of the services Randi provides include:

- Executive searches for positions such as Executive Director, CEO, CFO, Human Resource Director, etc.
  (see www.RandiFrank.com/category/executive-searches/);

- Conducting recruitment and testing for management, professional and clerical positions;
- Performing classification and salary studies, and preparing job descriptions;
- Preparing or revising personnel policies and Employee Handbooks;
- Conducting training on sexual harassment prevention; and
- Serving as an interim HR Manager as a contracted consultant.

Learn more and contact Randi:

Randi@RandiFrank.com

RandiFrank.com

LinkedIn.com/in/randifrankconsulting

Facebook.com/randifrankconsulting

203-213-3722

For articles on HR topics and sexual harassment prevention:

RandiFrank.com/blog

Chapter Seven

BELINDA GOODRICH

"Accomplishment Acceleration Through Micro Successes"

"There is so much to do and just not enough time to do it in!" How many times have you heard this or even uttered the same statement? We live in a world that moves faster than ever before, with increased demands to keep up and to compete, to be better and to do more. With so many balls in the air, is it surprising that many of those balls come crashing to the ground, leaving us feeling frustrated, defeated and discouraged?

In years past, our work was relatively predictable and repeatable. Employees were assigned a defined set of tasks and then were measured against the accomplishments of those tasks. Periodically, additional expectations may have been generated in response to an organizational need or project. Today's business environment, however, has been massively disrupted by technology and an ever-increasing pace of change. While this disruption propels companies and organizations in entirely new growth patterns, there is also a downside: Our stress levels are increasing while our self-confidence and overall job satisfaction is decreasing.

DISTRACTIONS = DISSATISFACTIONS

While we know communication is a necessary tool for business, our communication channels and communication options have become out-of-control. Historically, we would approach our communication exchanges deliberately: We'd pick up the phone to make a call or would write or read a letter. Deliberate communication has given way to a 24/7, always-on, constant stream of communication; emails clutter our inboxes and the continuous chime of our cell phone tempts our easily distracted brains. Fear of missing out (FOMO) compels us to constantly check our phones and scan our social media accounts. For many people, grabbing the cell phone has become the first movement of the day upon waking.

One email may prompt six other follow-up emails and looking at a text message on our phone may open the door, so to speak, to checking our social media sites. And that is when you slip down into the rabbit hole of distraction. This rabbit hole is especially damaging at work. Not only does it affect our job performance, it impacts and possibly erodes our relationships with our supervisors, peers and direct reports. The rabbit hole also lends to an increase in multitasking.

Albert Einstein once said, "Any man who can drive safely while kissing a pretty girl is simply not giving the kiss the attention it deserves."

Multi-tasking has become the prevailing way of life as we are pulled in all these directions. And how effective are you at multitasking? I can almost guarantee that you are not nearly as effective as you think you are. As Einstein so eloquently alluded to, when we split our attention between two or more tasks, we give neither task the attention it needs. Researchers at the University of California at Irvine found that "workers took an average of 25 minutes to recover from interruptions"[1] when returning to their original task. Task-switching disrupts work flow and results in lower-quality outputs.

The bigger issue is that when you are not making progress, you get frustrated, discouraged and disappointed. And that's when your negative self-talk begins — the nasty little voice in your head that tells you that you're not worthy of accomplishing the goals, you're incapable or other outright lies. Another common symptom of the lack of progress and goal attainment is imposter syndrome. Imposter syndrome is an attack of self-doubt in which you truly believe that you are not capable of the work, or not qualified for the job or task. Being spread too thin results in a lack of progress. This lack of progress feeds that imposter syndrome.

When we split our attention between two or more tasks, we give neither task the attention it needs.

MICROBITES OF SUCCESS

"... baby step onto the elevator ... baby step into the elevator ... I'm in the elevator."

– Bob Wiley, *What About Bob?*

The time has come to turn away from large, lofty goals and the "dream big" sentiments of the 20th century and focus instead on the small wins

---

1   Rosen, C. (2008). "The Myth of Multitasking." *The New Atlantis. A Journal of Technology and Society*, 105-110.

and the huge payback of microbites of success. This approach and these ideas originate from two areas of study: Adlerian theory and agile project management.

Alfred Adler was a cohort of Sigmund Freud, but instead of feeling that the root of psychosis was in the past, Adler had his patients look to the future. Adler worked with re-offending prisoners in the Vienna Prison System. Half of his patients underwent traditional or a Freudian-style therapy, discussing their past and their "mommy issues." Adler worked with the other half of the population on setting incremental goals.

These goals were broken into smaller increments, and each prisoner was tasked with working toward his goals via accountability sessions. The results were significant! Prisoners who participated in traditional therapy had minimal, if any, changes to their re-offense rate. However, Adler's goal-focused group not only began to accomplish the incremental goals they set, but the re-offending rate was greatly decreased. The human psyche loves to achieve goals! The drive to be productive and to succeed is fundamental.

Agile project management is a general term for a number of project management approaches that were originally applied to the software development field. Agile project management focuses on increased customer satisfaction and increased quality through frequent review, inspection and delivery of value-added increments of functionality. Agile approaches are adaptive processes that allow for changes and modifications throughout the project. The old mantra of project management was "plan the work and work the plan." This is not agile.

While working the plan may work in environments or situations where the work, the outcomes and the resources are stable and predictable, it is not effective in environments of change, volatility and shifting priorities. Agile breaks the work down into short "sprints" or "iterations," usually two to four weeks. At the end of each iteration, something is delivered or accomplished. The team focuses only on the work of that iteration. This approach limits the work-in-progress and sets incremental goals. After each iteration, the team examines what worked and what did not work, thus always improving their work habits and processes.

Combining an Adlerian approach to goal-setting and accountability with the concepts of agile project management allows employees hyper-focus on one task at a time. A bundle of tasks equates to the achievement of a short-term goal. Those short-term goals, in turn, feed our accomplishment roadmap. Collecting hash marks in the "win" column feeds our self-confidence, allowing us to truly understand that we are capable of amazing things. Distraction, shiny objects, the "squirrel-zone," imposter syndrome and FOMO can all be conquered: one microbite of success at a time. To understand how microbites of success work, we must first understand how our brain reacts to success and achievement.

The human psyche loves to achieve goals! The drive to be productive and to succeed is fundamental.

OUR BRAIN ON SUCCESS

When was the last time you celebrated a big achievement? Maybe it was a raise or a promotion; maybe it was running your first 5k race or half marathon; maybe it was graduating from college. How did you feel at that moment? Did you feel like you could take on the world? Did you give yourself, even for a moment, the recognition that you are an amazing, capable person? Those feelings and emotions are the result of a hormone surge in our brain. A beautiful thing happens in our brains upon goal accomplishment: A positive feedback mechanism is invoked that empowers and accelerates our drive for achievement. The more we achieve, the more we believe we can achieve.

The human body is an incredible machine and the intricate mechanisms at play allow us to grow, adapt, engage, survive, reproduce and thrive. For us to maintain homeostasis, our bodies employ both negative and positive feedback loops. A negative feedback loop looks for the "too much" message and then it will shut down the system or process. To understand a negative feedback loop, consider how insulin controls our blood sugar. When a person's blood sugar rises and hits a certain level as detected by receptors, the pancreas gets the signal to release insulin to lower that blood sugar. Once the level of blood sugar is homeostatic, the pancreas stops producing insulin. A negative feedback mechanism picks up that there is "too much" of something bad, so it sends a signal to release a remedy for that.

A positive feedback mechanism, in comparison, picks up that there is something good, so it triggers more of that good thing. It senses a stimulus and in reaction, enhances the original stimulus. When a woman goes into labor, for example, her body begins to produce oxytocin, which leads to contractions. This signals the body to continue to produce *more* oxytocin until the baby is born, which then terminates the cycle. This type of positive feedback can also occur within the "joy and pleasure" center of our brain. When we accomplish a goal, our body releases a cocktail of hormones that increases our happiness. In that happy state, we seek more of the stimulus that made us feel that pleasure: accomplishment.

ACCOMPLISHMENT ACCELERATION PROCESS

How do you step away from your multi-tasking and make things happen? You need to tap in to that positive feedback mechanism. To do that, you accelerate your accomplishments through practicing focused habits that yield micro successes! These micro successes not only yield consistent results, they give you a surge of "feel-good" hormones that bring more energy to the next task. Because the progress is incremental, you can change course and adapt as necessary.

Step 1 – Create the Picture: Picture your future! Where do you want to go? What do you want to be? Visualize that you are going to take a marvelous, twisting and turning journey to get to that destination. There will be up-hills, downhills, roadblocks and fast lanes, but they are all part of the landscape that makes up your individual journey. Progress is never a straight line! This picture may be within your current job role, or maybe it is a journey toward a promotion or a new job.

Progress is never a straight line!

Step 2 – List Your Short-Term Goals: With the destination in mind, create a list of high-level goals or accomplishments for the short-term that will be instrumental in accomplishing your journey. Ideally, the goals can be accomplished within a month or two. Be sure to make them specific and measurable. For example, "I will pursue my Master's degree by enrolling in classes at Grand Canyon University for the spring semester."

Step 3 – Choose Your Focused Goal: Select the one that is the most important to you. Be careful here! It is so easy to overestimate our time and energy and to select multiple goals. After all, we are in a "do-all, be-all" society. But remember, it's that very mentality that has caused us to burn out and not capture our full potential. For this process, you will want to choose just one goal. What goal are you most passionate about? Or maybe you choose one that is foundational to other goals. Whichever goal you identify as most important, be excited about it and be able to see what life looks like when that goal is accomplished.

Step 4 – Decompose the Goal: Now it's time to break that goal down into actionable tasks. What are all the components of the goal? What will need to happen for that goal to be fulfilled? Break the work of the goal into smaller pieces that can be accomplished in less than a week. Write down your list of tasks and enjoy the satisfaction of crossing them off as you get them done. Acknowledge your timeline and commitment. If this is a special project, allocate your time to it appropriately. For example, commit to spending 90 minutes per day only working on these tasks, one task at a time!

HINT: To stay focused and out of the rabbit hole, I recommend writing the tasks on a sticky note. Pull the sticky note of the task you are working on and commit to working on only that task until it is done. I put the sticky note right on the edge of my computer monitor as a constant reminder not to get distracted.

Step 5 – Microbites: Daily work should be broken down into micro-bites. Microbites are your small, quick wins. These wins fuel your feeling of accomplishment and supply you with a nice kick of adrenaline. [Courtney: If you use create a pull-quote from the preceding, modify the pull-quote so it says "Small, quick wins fuel your feeling of …"] Ideally your microbites should be small pieces of work that are accomplishable in 90 minutes or less. The key with the microbites is that they need to be done-done. Done-done means that we are going to accept them as done and not revisit them. This is especially important if you struggle with perfectionism. Sometimes done is better than perfect!

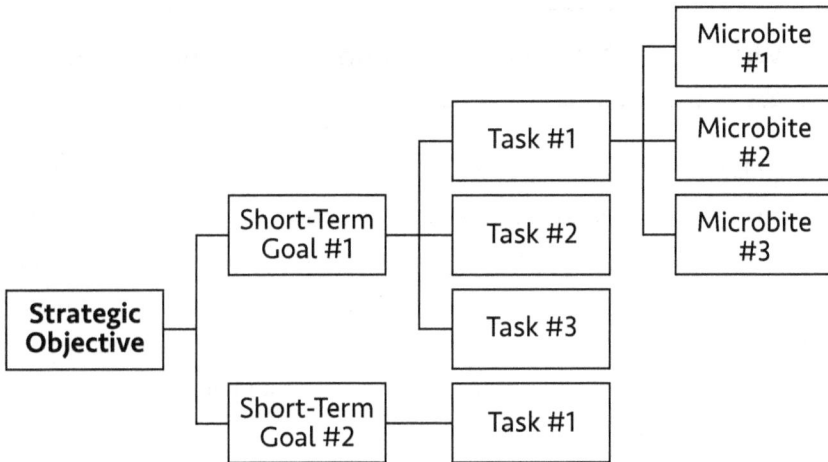

THE POWER-PACKED TRIO TO MICROSUCCESS: WRITE IT, SEE IT AND BE ACCOUNTABLE FOR IT

The accomplishment acceleration process works, but it takes time and commitment. Just like with any other habit or change, the more you do it, the easier it becomes. To continually reinforce the concepts: Write it, See it and Be Accountable for it!

Write it! If the introduction of the personal computer was a cupcake, smartphones are certainly the frosting on the top! Typing, keyboarding, texting, swiping and talk-to-text have replaced good old-fashioned pens and pencils. So why write when you can type? Because the act of writing creates new neural connections in our brains, allowing us to not only process information better, but to also retain and recall that information more quickly and more coherently. Writing a goal versus typing a goal is significantly more effective for putting that goal into our consciousness and the forefront of our thinking and motivation.

Writing creates new neural connections in our brains.

A popular trend for writing and tracking projects and progress is bullet journaling. A bullet journal refers to a notebook that may have dot grids versus lines, allowing the writer to format the pages however they desire. Bringing in colors, such as with colored pens, pencils or markers, can also make your goals and your progress more vivid in your mind. Whether you use a bullet journal, scratch paper, sticky notes or a Hello Kitty! notebook, the magic is in the writing.

See it! Seeing is believing. To truly be motivated, engaged and excited about the work we are taking on, we need to believe that we are going to accomplish it. Creating a vision map or some type of visual representation not only of the work we are doing but also our progress against that work goal is a visual reminder of what we are doing and why we are doing it. Vision mapping has become increasingly popular to counteract the constant bombardment of distractions. A fun technique is to electronically create a vision map and set it as the background on your phone and computer.

In agile project management, another visual tool leveraged is known as an iteration burndown chart. The burndown chart is a relatively simple graph showing how many hours are remaining in our work period as compared to how many estimated hours of *work* are left in our work period. Updated daily, the burndown chart gives us the picture of where we are, how we are performing and if we need to make any course corrections.

Be Accountable for It! We are the company we keep. With whom do you spend most of your time? The people around us fall into three categories: They are either lifting us up, pulling us down, or having little effect on us. Consider your friends, family members and co-workers — under which category do most of them fall? Seek out those people who lift you up, who challenge you and who propel you forward.

Self-organized masterminds and support groups are becoming popular, thanks, in part, to social media. Leveraging tools such as Slack, Zoom and Skype, you can utilize self-organized groups that can meet on a set basis, problem-solve, motivate and hold each other accountable. Another option is to find an accountability partner who has similar goals or objectives. We see this play out all the time in our personal lives: You agree to meet a friend before work to go for a run. While your comfortable bed may seem like a better option early in the morning, the fact that you know your friend is waiting for you compels you to lace up and head out the door. Who in your life will hold you accountable?

CONCLUSION

We have all been given this beautiful gift of life and we have a choice, at every moment of this life, as to how we are going to live it and what we are going to accomplish. You hold your future in your hands. It is amazing what you can accomplish when you put the phone down, shut off the distractions and just work at being the amazing YOU that YOU are!

ABOUT THE AUTHOR

Belinda Goodrich
PMP, PgMP, PMI-SP, PMI-RMP, PMI-ACP, CAPM, CSM

Globally recognized as a project management expert, Belinda Goodrich is the founder and CEO of The Goodrich Institute and PM Learning Solutions. PM Learning Solutions is focused on delivering world-class project management exam preparation programs and materials. Through The Goodrich Institute, Belinda serves as a consultant to several Fortune 500 companies with a focus on improving the project management processes and practices in order to drive business growth.

After more than 20 years of corporate project management and executive leadership experience, Belinda "retired" to serve the project management community. The first woman in the world to achieve five of the PMI credentials, Belinda now holds the following: PMP, CAPM, PMI-SP, PMI-ACP, PMI-RMP, PgMP. In addition, Belinda is a Certified Scrum Master.

With a focus on industrial and organizational psychology, Belinda is fascinated with the mind, emotions and behaviors of project managers and stakeholders, and she leverages that fascination to bring practical application to project management techniques.

The author of multiple books and courseware on project management and PMI exam topics, Belinda is an in-demand facilitator, speaker and consultant. As an instructor, Belinda has helped thousands of project managers achieve their project management credentials. Her passion is creating the connection between theoretical project management concepts and real-world business needs through energetic and engaging sessions.

Belinda holds a BA in behavior science, as well as an MBA, from Western International University. She is currently pursuing her MS in psychology, with a focus on industrial and organizational psychology, from Grand Canyon University.

Originally from Maine, Belinda now resides in Arizona with her husband and three rescue dogs. Belinda's ever-expanding brood includes three daughters and six grandchildren! She started running just a few years ago and has completed three marathons.

Learn more and contact Belinda:

Belinda@PMLearningSolutions.com

Facebook.com/PMBelindaSpeaks

Twitter.com/PMBelindaSpeaks

Linkedin.com/in/BelindaGoodrich

BelindaGoodrich.com

888-871-7657

Chapter Eight

MICHELE FANTT HARRIS

"Transitioning into Retirement"

Recently, I received the following announcements from friends telling me of their pending retirements:

> "After 16+ wonderful years with the ABC Company and more than 30 years in Human Resources, I am retiring on March 30! I am very excited about this next stage in my life, and my husband I have had this planned for two years. Time has flown by!"

> "After 30 years at XYZ Company, I will be leaving next month and moving to Florida. My family has requested that I move closer. This is a very challenging and scary time for me. Please keep in touch!"

The first retiree planned her retirement for two years and was very excited about her transition to retirement. The other retiree was reluctantly retiring and moving away from friends and colleagues. She knows that this next stage in her life will be challenging, and she's also scared and appears to have very few plans for what she will be doing next.

Retirement means many things to different people. Some people welcome getting their "gold watch" and settling into a world of leisure without deadlines or any daily demands. Others want to remain active and plan to pursue their dreams or passions, such as learning to play the piano, learning a new language or taking a cruise around the world. Some people want to stay engaged in the workplace but choose to change careers — they may start a new business or turn their avocation into a new vocation. Many employees who would *like* to retire are forced to keep working after age 65 due to the increased costs of healthcare, rising living costs and inadequate retirement savings.

Retirement doesn't have to be a scary time for employees, but should be a time of careful planning and reflecting.

A TIME OF CAREFUL PLANNING AND REFLECTING, AND HOW EMPLOYERS CAN HELP

The U.S. Census reported that only 19.3% of people age 65 and older were in the labor force in 2016. It projects that by 2026, 21.8% of the workforce will be people age 65 or older.

Retirement doesn't have to be a scary time for employees, but should be a time of careful planning and reflecting. Employers can help employees ease into retirement by offering a number of pre-retirement benefits to prepare employees for the next phase of their lives.

Take, for example, my organization. At National Cooperative Bank, N.A. (NCB), the average age of our employees is 42. We hire experienced employees who are mid to late in their banking careers. Realizing that

we may lose 10% of staff in the next few years, we offered retirement
planning courses called Retirewise through MetLife Insurance Company.
We selected the courses that appealed the most to our employee popu-
lation and offered these classes during a four-week period: Build the
Foundation, Creating and Managing Wealth, Establishing Retirement
Income, and Maximizing What You Have.

**"Allowing employees to move from full-time to part-time
status in the final year before their retirement benefits
the employer because it helps the organization improve
workplace planning and succession planning, and helps
facilitate the transfer of institutional knowledge."**

For employees who are considering retirement in a year or less, we allow
employees to move from full-time to part-time status. Employees are
allowed to reduce their work hours but continue to be paid at the same
hourly rate. This flexible retirement benefit allows employees to ease into
retirement while maintaining their work identity and exploring retirement options before making a complete break from the workplace. This
option benefits the Bank because it helps us improve our workplace planning and succession planning, and helps facilitate the transfer of institutional knowledge. Employees are gradually able to train and transition
projects to employees who are less senior in their roles, and do so at their
pace as opposed to being forced to transition the work when they give
notice. Employees to whom the work is being handed off are able to ask
questions and clarify new work assignments while the retiring worker is
still there to give direct feedback about the work task. This type of phased
or gradual retirement process is really beginning to catch on, across many
industries and in various types of organizations. Some federal government agencies, for example, provide phased retirement programs to their

potential retirees. In the phased retirement program, employees are able to reduce their work week to 20 hours per week. Ten of the 20 hours are spent mentoring their replacements, while the remaining 20 hours allows the employees to continue working their regular jobs. As for their compensation, if employees would like to continuing earning 100% of their salary while working 20 hours a week, they can have the remaining half of their salary come from their retirement annuity. Employees may continue in the phased retirement program for up to three years before actually leaving their government job.

Employers should consider hiring retirees as consultants or brand ambassadors.

In addition to providing a transition year for retiring employees, companies can also consider the continuation or partial continuation of employee benefits for its retirees. Again, take my organization as an example. One of the fringe benefits that the Bank offers its employees and retirees is consumer banking services. Employees can earn an extra one percent of interest on savings accounts and certificates of deposits. Employees are able to continue this valuable benefit after retirement, providing that their years of service to the Bank combined with their age equal 70 (e.g., if a retire is 57 and worked for the bank for at least 13 years). This extended additional interest on savings accounts allows retiring employees to continue to increase their retirement savings and allows them to feel that they are still a part of the NCB family. This benefit is extremely helpful in today's economy, when the average savings account pays less than 1% interest.

Access to ample savings is no smaller matter for today's retirees. With retirees living longer and healthcare costs rising, many are fearful that they will exhaust their savings during their retirement. In a 2016 retirement survey conducted by Transamerica Center for Retirement Studies, 43% of the surveyed workers over age 50 were fearful of outliving their savings and investments. This fear ranks higher than declining health and loneliness.

LEVERAGING THE EVOLVING NEEDS AND TALENTS OF RETIREES AND MATURE WORKERS

Today's mature workers aren't retiring in the way their parents did, but are instead seeking ways to find meaning and purpose in their lives. They are looking to remain productive and engaged after they leave the company. This is great news for companies! Employers should consider hiring retirees as consultants or brand ambassadors. Hiring a retiree as a consultant to do the work that you know he or she can perform saves the company money and time. You don't have to advertise or recruit an unknown consultant. You know your retirees, their work experience and their work ethic. You know that your retirees can hit the ground running and do an excellent job for you. Retirees need little training or orientation, as they know the work environment and the work expectations. They can return an accurate and proficient project in less time than a new consultant who doesn't know your organization or its processes.

Retirees also make excellent brand ambassadors for your company because they know the brand and identify with your mission. Employers should consider hiring retirees to represent the company at trade shows and conferences. Retirees know your product and service well, and can sell customers on the company's brand. A retiree represents a seasoned professional who knows the product and service and can sell it to new and existing clients.

Not every retiree, however, wants major responsibility or time-consuming commitments after he or she has transitioned to retired life. In our business, a retiree will occasionally tell us they don't want a project that requires travel or anything too challenging. I usually call these retirees for temporary clerical assignments at the Bank. I've used retirees to help with fulfilling a mailing assignment or to serve as the temporary receptionist. Retirees can also fill in for regular employees who are on FMLA leave, vacation or sabbaticals. Retirees get to return to the workplace and connect with former colleagues, as well as earn extra income without the pressures of a long-term commitment or project assignment. This type of relationship between employer and retirees is win-win for everyone.

KEEP INVESTING IN MATURE WORKERS, ALL THE WAY TO RETIREMENT

It's vital to keep investing in your mature workers as they approach retirement. My organization, NCB, invests in employees at every stage of their careers. Educational assistance is just one example. We use this fringe benefit to provide up to $5,250 per year in tuition reimbursement to each employee who chooses to take advantage of it. Employees have used the educational assistance program to take courses or training seminars that will assist them professionally on the job or for a future opportunity in their retirement. The educational assistance benefits can help a pre-retiree write a chapter in a book or do research in a new field of study. Others used educational assistance funds to pursue a new degree that will be used to help them in their current role as well as their next career or retiree endeavor. I have found that pre-retirees are so grateful for the benefit offered to them that they are more dedicated than the average worker and give beyond the call of duty on their regular jobs.

NCB's Human Resources office also conducts an annual career development workshop that provides a process and a set of tools to develop or renew an employee's career plan. The focus of the workshop is on an employee's personal and professional growth and development. Some of the employees use the career development workshop tools to plan for their retirement. In the workshop, we help employees discover their talents — activities or work experiences that they find satisfying and that they excel at. Hopefully, these talents will provide an insight to a new job opportunity at the Bank, but it might provide an insight to a future retirement endeavor.

The more aligned your values are with your work or retirement endeavors, the more satisfied and fulfilling your retirement will be.

Also, we ask the career development workshop participants to identify their values. Values are the beliefs that they hold most dear. Values determine what is important and meaningful to you and provide a roadmap to one's lifetime decisions and choices. These values guide you in your future plans. Research shows the more aligned your values are with your work or retirement endeavors, the more satisfied and fulfilling your retirement will be. Workshop participants who are preparing for retirement are able to define personal and professional development opportunities that they want to pursue after they leave the Bank. Participants are able to address: How does my current role at the Bank or future retirement endeavor align with my core values? Are there job assignments, volunteer opportunities or other activities that align well with my values? How do I prepare myself for a future role that aligns with my personal values? See the final section of this chapter for a list of values you and your employees may find helpful in doing this type of exploration. Does your organization provide professional development experiences for employees who are preparing to retire? Or do you mistakenly think that retirees don't need or deserve this type of fringe benefit as they are headed out the door? Preparing for "what's next" is something that all employees — at all ages and at all stages in their career — need. And providing those opportunities for planning or personal insight are good for the organization too.

As for outplacement services and career coaches, many organizations don't think to offer them to retirees. But whether the employee is ready to embark on a new career or retirement, these services are invaluable. Outplacement services are typically provided to employees who are involuntarily terminated because of a job misfit or a reduction in force, but outplacement services provide the necessary tools to help an employee define their career goals and career path and help them move to a more satisfying career. Also, career coaches can assist employees with in-depth retirement self-assessments designed to surface unique retirement motivators and special considerations. Career coaches help employees think outside of the traditional retirement model. As mature-age employees consider alternative options — like serving on a board of directors, starting a business or volunteering their time — a career coach can bridge the gap by focusing an employee on his or her applicable skills and personal values to guide them to their next venture.

As mature-age employees consider alternative options — like serving on a board of directors, starting a business or volunteering their time — a career coach can bridge the gap by focusing an employee on his or her applicable skills and personal values to guide them to their next venture.

In the end, the employers that provide support and assistance at every phase of an employee's career — even during retirement planning and well into retirement — will be the organizations that remain competitive in a job seeker's market. When employees (young or old, new or seasoned) are provided with continuing education, career coaching, flexible schedules, and financial opportunities and career transition services, those employees will gain the skills required to perform at their best for your company. By investing in the whole employee experience — from day one on the new job to the employee's retirement day — employers are creating a win-win relationship. Employees are committed to their employer during their employment and ultimately are likely to serve as goodwill ambassadors for the organization during retirement.

*   *   *

WHAT ARE MY VALUES?[1]

Values are the beliefs that ground you and are very special to you personally. Your values determine what is important and meaningful to you; they guide your decisions in your career, in your relationships and in your life.

As such, understanding your values is vital. This exercise can help you to do that.

Directions: Rate each value on a scale of 1 to 5, with a 5 meaning that the value is extremely important to you and a 1 meaning that it is not very important to you. Then look at your rankings to identify your top five values (probably items that you scored with a 5 or a 4).

---

1   This exercise is used with permission of its developer, Lynn Ware of Integral Talent Systems. A version of this exercise appears in the participant guide and learning journal for the ITS program "Talent Match: Navigating Your Career." www.itsinc.net

_____ **Building a Better World:** Doing something that contributes to improving the world we live in.

_____ **Helping Others:** Becoming directly involved in helping other people, either individually or in small groups.

_____ **Winning by Competing:** Engaging in activities that pit your abilities against others.

_____ **Influencing People:** Influencing the attitudes or opinions of other people.

_____ **Learning New Things:** Having freedom to engage in the pursuit of knowledge and understanding.

_____ **Becoming the Best in My Field:** Achieving mastery in whatever work you do.

_____ **Being Able to Express Myself Creatively:** Engaging in creative artistic expression.

_____ **Having a Beautiful Environment:** Creating or surrounding yourself with a beauty that you can appreciate and enjoy.

_____ **Having Lots of Variety:** Engaging in work activities that frequently change.

_____ **Receiving Recognition:** Receiving recognition for the high quality of your work.

_____ **Having Excitement and Adventure:** Experiencing a high degree of (or frequent) excitement in the course of your work and having work duties that require frequent risk-taking.

____ **Making Lots of Money:** Achieving great monetary rewards for your work.

____ **Being Physically Active:** Using your physical capabilities in your work.

____ **Having Autonomy and Freedom:** Determining the nature of your work without significant direction from others.

____ **Moral Integrity:** Engaging in work that maintains a set of moral standards that you feel are very important.

____ **Having a Community at Work:** Being a part of a team that helps each other and sometimes shares activities outside of work.

____ **Work/Life Balance:** Meeting your work responsibilities in a timeframe that matches with other priority activities in your life.

____ **Having Stability and Job Security:** Establishing work routine and job duties that are largely predictable. Feeling assured of keeping your job and receiving satisfactory compensation.

____ **Other:** _____

ABOUT THE AUTHOR

Michele Fantt Harris

SHRM-SCP, SPHR, ACC

Michele Fantt Harris is the Executive Vice President, Human Resources, for the National Cooperative Bank in Washington, D.C. A seasoned HR professional, Michele has worked in human resources in the education, nonprofit, healthcare, and the finance and insurance industries.

This is Michele's fourth professional anthology: To read her previous books, check out *What's Next in Human Resources* (Greyden Press 2015), *Rethinking Human Resources* (Red Letter Publishing 2015), *Evolution of Human Resources* (Red Letter Publishing 2016) and *Humans@Work* (Red Letter Publishing 2017).*

Michele is active in many human resources organizations, and is past president of the Human Resources Association of the National Capital Area and the former Black Human Resources Network. She has been a member of the Society for Human Resource Management since 1985, served on the Society for Human Resource Management national board from 1996 through 2001 and is a past chair of the SHRM Foundation Board of Directors.

Michele is an Associate Certified Coach (ACC) through the International Coach Federation and a Certified Career Management

---

* Books originally published by Red Letter Publishing became part of the Silver Tree Publishing catalog in 2017 through an asset acquisition.

Coach (CCMC) through The Academies, Inc. A member of Delta Sigma Theta Sorority, Inc., she served on the board of the Delta Research and Educational Foundation from 2008 to 2014. Michele currently serves on the Board of Regents for the Leadership Center for Excellence.

Michele received her Bachelor of Arts degree from the University of Maryland, Baltimore County; a Master of Administrative Science from Johns Hopkins University; and her Juris Doctorate from the University of Baltimore School of Law. A certified Senior Professional in Human Resources (SPHR) and Global Professional in Human Resources (GPHR), Michele teaches at Prince Georges Community College and Catholic University.

Michele is a native of Baltimore, Maryland, and currently resides with her husband in the District of Columbia with their rescue Brittany Spaniel canine kid.

Learn more and contact Michele:

MFHarris@ncb.coop

Michele.Harris19@gmail.com

Chapter Nine

ALICIA K. LAMBERT

"Propel Your Career with Employee Engagement"

Employee engagement has been a hot topic in the business world for well over two decades. The Gallup organization, experts in employee engagement, have studied and measured employee engagement for more than 35 years. Their employee engagement survey has been administered to more than 195,600 U.S. companies and their Q^{12} Client Database currently contains more than 31 million respondents. Through their research, Gallup has found that organizations with high engagement outperform their peers that have lower engagement on every metric from revenue and productivity to safety and absenteeism.

Highly engaged employees are not only more productive, creative, innovative and successful, but they also are happier, healthier and have better overall well-being than their counterparts. By taking ownership of your career with a focus on proven strategies to increase engagement, you can and will unleash your potential to propel your career. Don't worry if your company doesn't have an employee engagement initiative. In this chapter, I'll share strategies that are for anyone who wants to create a competitive advantage and distinguish themselves from the crowd.

WHAT IS ENGAGEMENT?

Gallup defines engaged employees as "those who are involved in, enthusiastic about and committed to their work and workplace." Employee engagement is the "degree to which employees are involved in and enthusiastic about their work and workplace." All employees fall into one of three categories of engagement.

1. **Engaged**: People who have a passion for their work and workplace. They are creative, innovative, and actively look for ways to drive performance and make the organization better.

2. **Not Engaged**: People who get the job done but have no passion or energy for their work and often do just enough to get by. They have little to no connection to the work and/or the organization and are usually biding their time until another job comes along

3. **Actively Disengaged**: People who actively work to destroy their peers, teams, and/or the company. They are unhappy and actively invite others to share in their misery. They also underperform their engaged peers in nearly every measurable dimension.

Actively disengaged employees are unhappy and actively invite others to share in their misery. They also underperform their engaged peers.

Engaged employees distinguish themselves from their peers with purpose and achievement. They are resilient, tenacious, determined and bring high energy to their work. Not only do they work with a sense of pride, but they also inspire others with their enthusiasm. Engaged employees and teams are more productive, profitable and customer-focused, and they experience less turnover and produce superior work — all qualities that every company desires.

WHY DOES DISENGAGEMENT MATTER?

Disengagement is expensive! Since 2000 when Gallup began tracking engagement, there has been no significant improvement in the percentage of engaged employees in the U.S. Currently, only 33% of the U.S. working population is engaged. Disengaged employees comprise 51% of the population and the rest, 16%, are actively disengaged — costing U.S. employers between $483 to $605 billion each year in lost productivity. Companies with high Q^{12} scores experience 41% lower absenteeism, 17% higher productivity, 20% higher sales, 10% higher customer metrics, 21% higher profitability, and between 24% to 59% lower turnover than companies with lower scores. Engaged employees are the key to sustainable organizational success.

Why should this matter to you? There is a significant relationship between engagement and individual performance. Engaged employees are rare, they stand out, and companies value what they bring to the table because they deliver better and more sustainable results than non-engaged employees. Engagement is a competitive advantage gamechanger.

As you look to progress in your career, you will need to distinguish yourself from others. An estimated 10,000 Baby Boomers are retiring every day and 47% of people say that now is a good time to find a better or higher paying job. More people looking for jobs means more competition, inside and outside of organizations. Utilizing engagement as a career development strategy is a strategic re-framing that can help you get and keep the job of your dreams.

THE ENGAGEMENT STRATEGY

Let's use Gallup's 12 "Q^{12}" questions — a proven framework for assessing engagement among a company's employees — as a starting point for developing an "engagement strategy" that you can use in your job and your career to help you outperform the competition and to be more satisfied every day at work. What follows is a detailed set of tips around the 12 engagement dimensions, with explanations of how you can know whether you're performing well in this regard and with specific, actionable advice on how to improve.

In the end, if you achieve all 12 outcomes (by ultimately saying "yes" to each of the statements below), you'll be in a unique and rare position — more highly engaged than most American workers and ready to wow your colleagues and enjoy your work in a way you have never before done.

Let's get started getting more engaged!

Basic Needs

Q1: I know what is expected of me at work.

This foundational question sets the stage for all other elements of engagement. Companies employ people not only to do work, but to deliver results. If we are unsure of expectations, confusion can lead to frustration, conflict and ultimately disengagement. Below are three specific ways to ensure you know what is expected of you at work.

✓ Clarify expectations.
  – Schedule regular check-ins with your leader to gain clarity on what is expected of you daily, including both implicit and explicit

expectations. Your job description may read differently than the work you do every day — never assume, always ask.

✓ Understand the big picture.

✓ How does your work fit in to the overall vision for your team and the organization? How does your work align with the organization's goals? If your work does not align, ask yourself why you are doing it? Work with your leader to understand your work in the context of your team, department, and organization. Participate in goal setting.

– Only 30% of people say their manager involves them in setting their goals at work — be one of those people. Be proactive by creating two or three goals prior to meeting with your manager. Make sure your goals highlight your understanding of not only your own work, but how your work impacts the team and organization. Utilize the strategy for your team/department, business unit and organization in creating your goals. What does outstanding performance look like? Ask for specific examples and adjust your goals accordingly.

Only 30% of people say their manager involves them in setting their goals at work — be one of those people.

By taking a proactive approach to understanding your job expectations, you not only set yourself up for success, but also communicate to your leadership that you are serious about your professional development and career.

📖 Great Reads

- *So Good They Can't Ignore You* by Cal Newport
- *Start with Why* by Simon Sinek
- *Seeing the Big Picture: Business Acumen to Build Your Credibility, Career, and Company* by Kevin Cope

---

Q2: I have the materials and equipment I need to do my work right.

What do you need to stand out as a top performer? Materials and equipment may also include *people* you need to connect with to gain information and influence your work. Consider these four steps for getting there:

✓ Plan for your success.

    – Develop a plan for how you will achieve your goals. Utilize process improvement skills like Six Sigma or Project Management to craft your plan.

✓ Ask for what you need.

    – This may seem like common sense, but common sense isn't always common practice. Identify key stakeholders who are invested in your success and involve them in your planning. Share your plan and ask for their feedback and support.

✓ Create a business case.

    – How will gaining the resources you need to be successful help the team and organization be successful? Aligning your needs with the needs of the organization creates a compelling argument for your position and increases the likelihood that you will receive what you need. Before stating your case, ensure you have a solid understanding of your team and organization's big picture.

✓ Be resourceful.

- You may not get exactly what you need to do your work right, but don't allow that to impede your ability to do what you can do well. What resources do you have at your disposal? Who do you know who may be willing to share knowledge, resources or materials? What do you have to offer that you can barter for what you need?

Individual Needs

Q3: At work, I have the opportunity to do what I do best every day.

The difference between loving and dreading work is what you do when you get there. It's easy for people to become disengaged when their natural talents are not aligned with their work. Poor job fit can lead to poor performance, boredom and potentially to termination. Try these three key strategies for making sure you get to do your best work, every day.

The difference between loving and dreading work is what you do when you get there.

✓ Discover your strengths.

- What comes easily to you? What parts of your job, if removed, would cause you to become devastated or disengaged?

- List what you love about your work that you want to continue to do and those things you would not miss if they were taken away. Request work that aligns with your strengths and recommend aligning other work with the strengths of your team members.

– Increase your self-awareness by taking personality and/or behavioral assessments. Some of the more common assessments include StrengthsFinder, DiSC and MBTI. Remember that these assessments offer a snapshot into who you are and how you behave; they in no way define you or should limit you.

– Ask family, friends, peers, and former and current leaders for feedback. Past performance reviews are a great resource.

✓ Develop your strengths.

– Become an expert at something. The well-rounded person is a myth; stars don't have round edges — they have points.

– Read books, take a class, utilize in-house training and eLearning, or get an advanced degree — don't leave tuition reimbursement money on the table.

✓ Maintain a healthy lifestyle.

– Burnout is real and can affect your ability to be your best. Healthy eating and physical activity improve your ability to think, problem-solve, innovate, come back from setbacks and so much more.

Become an expert at something. The well-rounded person is a myth; stars don't have round edges — they have points.

📖 Great Reads

- *StrengthsFinder 2.0* by Tom Rath
- *Getting Things Done* by David Allen
- *Linchpin: Are You Indispensable?* by Seth Godin
- *Flow* by Mihaly Csikszentmihalyi

Q4: In the past seven days, I have received recognition or praise for doing good work.

This is one of the elements of engagement that you have less control over, but it doesn't mean you have no control. Try these three strategies for attracting the recognition you deserve.

✓ Promote yourself.

- Your leader knows that the work got done, but may not know what it took to get the work done. Keep your leader informed about the status of your projects and deliverables. Give them what they need to sing your praises to other leaders in the organization.

- Keep a "kudos" file with achievements and congratulations for a job well done. This will make it easier to highlight your achievements when it comes time for formal performance reviews.

✓ Be the change.

- Give what you want to others. Feedback doesn't have to just come from your leader. Recognize the great work of your leader and peers to encourage an environment of praise and recognition for all.

✓ Develop your own reward system.

　– Recognition doesn't and shouldn't always come from other people. Take time to celebrate and give yourself rewards for achieving your goals at work

---

📕 Great Reads

Drive: The Surprising Truth About What Motivates Us
by Dan Pink

Q5: My supervisor, or someone at work, seems to care about me as a person.

While you can't make people like you or care about you, you can show them you care about them. Try this:

✓ Show you care about others.

　– Invest in relationships that you care about. Get to know other people and invite them to get to know you as a person. Share personal information appropriately and be open to having meaningful connections at work.

Q6: There is someone at work who encourages my development.

People invest in those who show initiative and potential. Here are three ways to demonstrate that:

✓ Get a mentor — a trusted person to offer advice, share wisdom and tell you the hard truths. Listen and learn from their experience, there's no need to re-create the wheel.

✓ Find a sponsor to promote and showcase you within your organization, industry and/or community.

✓ Share your goals and progress.

   – Create an Individual Development Plan (IDP) for yourself. Include both personal and professional goals and share with your leader, mentor and sponsor.

"When employees' needs are met, they don't just become "happier," they become better performers."

  – Gallup, 2017 "State of the American Workplace"

Teamwork Needs

Q7: At work, my opinions seem to count.

You only have one time to make a first impression, so make it count! Try these two approaches:

✓ Speak up but temper your input.

   – Share your opinions; people can't read your mind. But speak only when you have something to add, not just to hear yourself talk.

✓ Think before you speak.

   – Steven Covey gave great advice when he said to "Seek first to understand, then to be understood." You offer greater value when you understand the full context and perspective of the situation before sharing your opinion.

📖 Great Reads

- *Emotional Intelligence 2.0* by Travis Bradberry and Jean Greaves
- *Mindset: The New Psychology of Success* by Carol Dweck
- *A More Beautiful Question: The Power of Inquiry to Spark Breakthrough Ideas* by Warren Berger
- *Influence: The Psychology of Persuasion* by Robert B. Cialdini
- *7 Habits of Highly Effective People* by Stephen R. Covey

Q8: The mission or purpose of my company makes me feel my job is important.

Learning more about your organization increases your business acumen and helps connect you to the mission, vision and purpose. In your learning, start with these two areas:

✓ Alignment of values.

- Connect your personal values with those of your organization. Where is the overlap? How does the work you do contribute to the organization's mission and vision?

✓ Making $$$.

- Develop your business acumen by learning how your company makes money. Who does what from start to finish? How does your work impact your team, other departments, and the customer or end user?

📖 **Great Reads**

- *What the CEO Wants You to Know* by Ram Charan
- *Good to Great* by Jim Collins

Q9: My associates or fellow employees are committed to doing quality work.

As the adage goes, "there's no 'I' in team." Working on a team where not everyone carries their fair share can lead to resentment and disengagement. Try these two approaches to surrounding yourself with teammates who are as committed as you are:

✓ Be supportive.

  – Partner with newer or less-skilled peers and offer support. Position yourself as the subject matter expert (SME) for your team and invest in their success.

✓ Be accountable.

  – Hold yourself and your team members accountable to the goals of the team. Use caution when giving feedback that should come from your leader, but don't avoid having conversations about behavior or actions that affect your ability to do excellent work.

Q10: I have a best friend at work.

Your *best* friend may be a childhood playmate or your college roommate, but it doesn't mean you can't have trusting relationships at work. Here are two ideas for how to make that possible:

✓ Be a best friend.

- Be reliable, trustworthy, and deliver quality work.
- Attend social events and encourage opportunities for your team to get together.

✓ Network, network, NETWORK.

- Development partnerships with peers across the business, and spend time investing in these relationships.
- Offer more than just your open hand. What can you do for the other people in your network?

📕 Great Reads

- *Never Eat Alone* by Keith Ferrazzi
- *How to Win Friends & Influence People* by Dale Carnegie

Growth Needs

Q11: In the past six months, someone at work has talked to me about my progress.

Feedback is one of the most valuable tools you have for your professional development and success. Here are some ideas on how to get the feedback you need and deserve:

✓ *Ask* for the feedback.

- What did you do well? What can you improve upon? While "great job" may feel good, it's not actionable and it's not repeatable. Seek feedback that you can apply immediately as you take steps to reach your goals.

   – Initiate discussions with your leader about your IDP and progress toward your goals. These should be at least monthly for formal feedback and weekly for informal feedback.

Q12: This past year, I have had opportunities at work to learn and grow.

Success is as success does. How can you hardwire your work experience for learning and growth? Here's how:

✓ Take responsibility for your growth.

   – Take on new projects and expansion opportunities as they are presented. Shift from "It's not my job" to "What can I learn?" and "How will this help me achieve my goals?"

   – Seek out opportunities through your network, mentor and sponsor.

   – Mentor other team members.

   – Move. Not every step has to be a step up. But movement is key. Expansion opportunities or lateral moves are a fantastic way to get exposure to other areas of the business, build your skills and showcase yourself.

▰ Great Reads

- *Give and Take: Why Helping Others Drives Our Success* by Adam Grant
- *Act Like a Leader, Think Like a Leader* by Herminia Ibarra
- *Lean In* by Sheryl Sandberg
- *Grit: The Power of Passion and Perseverance* by Angela Duckworth

NOTE: Whether you're using these questions and the engagement tips offered here to create your own career edge or to help members of your work team get and stay more engaged, be sure to focus your attentions first on the first six questions. They represent the basic and individual needs of engagement and are key to building overall engagement. Without a solid foundation, individuals and teams will find it more difficult to successfully engage with the last six questions.

CHOOSE ENGAGEMENT

Engagement is a choice — one that with the right strategy, can unleash your potential and propel your career.

Review the elements of engagement above — more than once and on more than one day — and think about what it would take for you to strongly agree with each item. Identify areas where your engagement is strong and others where it is weak; consider a red/yellow/green assessment of where you're doing well, where you're struggling and where you're just "okay." Then list three areas that would have the greatest impact on your overall engagement and career success; focus on *these* items for the next six months.

Being engaged at work isn't just about your company or your boss creating an engaging experience *for* you. Engagement, in many ways, is up to you. So, ask yourself:

What habits — good and bad — will promote or diminish my engagement?

Who do I need to be in order to increase my engagement?

What support do I need?

What does success look like?

Choosing engagement is a radical first step in a disengaged world. By creating your personalized engagement strategy and sharing it with others, you'll be taking bold and powerful responsibility for your engagement and opening yourself up to unforetold success. I wish you the greatest career possible.

Engagement is a choice — one that with the right strategy, can unleash your potential and propel your career.

References

McFarlane, Trish. "Owning Engagement in Your Workplace." Blog.SHRM.org, 16 Jan. 2017, blog.shrm.org/blog/owning-engagement-in-your-workplace.

Royal, Ken and Sorenson, Susan. "Employees Are Responsible for Their Engagement Too." News.Gallup.com, 16 Jun. 2015, http://news.gallup.com/business-journal/183614/employees-responsible-engagement.aspx.

Emond, Larry. "2 Reasons Why Employee Engagement Programs Fall Short" News.Gallup.com, 15 Aug. 2017, http://news.gallup.com/opinion/gallup/216155/reasons-why-employee-engagement-programs-fall-short.aspx.

The Gallup Organization. (2017). 2017 State of the American Workplace. Washington D.C.: The Gallup Organization.

Interested in asking Gallup's Q12 engagement questions to your team or organization? Learn more at https://q12.gallup.com/Public/en-us/Features.

ABOUT THE AUTHOR

Alicia K. Lambert
ACC, SHRM-SCP

Alicia K. Lambert is a leadership coach and consultant who helps leaders and professionals thrive by harnessing the limitless power of the brain. Through her boutique organization and leadership consulting firm, LeadershipING, she works with small and mid-size organizations to accelerate growth and drive business outcomes through high-performing, effective leaders.

With more than 15 years' experience as a human resource leader and leadership consultant in Fortune 500 and Global 500 organizations, Alicia has experience within the healthcare, manufacturing and technology industries working with organizations including Colgate-Palmolive, Bosch and Humana, Inc.

Alicia coaches physician and healthcare Executive MBA students with the Haslam College of Business at the University of Tennessee and facilitates continuing development leadership development programs at the University of Tennessee Conferences and Non-Credit Programs.

Alicia holds a Senior Human Resource Professional (SHRM-SCP) credential with the Society of Human Resource Management and is an Associate Certified Coach with the International Coach Federation. She is very involved in the Tennessee Valley Human Resource Association and Smoky Mountain Association of Talent

Development, and serves as the President of the International Coach Federation East Tennessee Sub-chapter.

Alicia was featured as an author in the 2015 *What's Next in Human Resources* Anthology (Greyden Press).

She received her bachelor's degree from the University of Tennessee, and completed the Co-Active coach training program through the Coaches Training Institute. She resides in Knoxville, Tennessee, with her senior pup, Pepper, and enjoys nature walks, crafting with glitter and rhinestones, and spending time with her nieces and nephews. She is a self-confessed book-hoarder and is spends most of her time researching neuroscience and human behavior.

Learn more and contact Alicia:

Alicia@AliciaKLambert.com

www.AliciaKLambert.com

www.Twitter.com/leadership_ING

www.Facebook.com/LeadershipING1

865-407-0017

Chapter Ten

NANCY LITTLE, PHD

"Come Alive to Fully Thrive as an Energy Creator®"

"Don't ask what the world needs! Ask what makes YOU come alive, and go do it. Because what the world needs are people who have come alive!"

– Howard Thurman

Turn within for a moment and ponder the question, "What do I need to call forth in order to be fully alive?" Perhaps you identified a specific word, such as courage, boldness or imagination.

On the other hand, you may have envisioned a person — possibly a mentor or a well-known leader — for whom you hold high regard. If so, reflect on the qualities that you most admire in them.

At a deeper level of contemplation, consider this: "Do I possess the passion, the desire and the willingness to accelerate my life, even if that means stepping outside of my safety zone to make my next brave move?"

"Courage is the main quality of leadership, in my opinion, no matter where it is exercised. Usually it implies some risk — especially in new undertakings."

– Walt Disney

As a leader, you carry an obligation to know how to create and manage the energy you need to succeed! The individuals who report to you, as well as the ones who supervise you, reap either positive benefits or negative consequences from the energy you emit in the workplace.

In your leadership role, you hold a position filled with opportunities to inspire others to more fully develop their innate potential in order to thrive. You can be a difference maker to those around you as they seek meaning and examine how their lives matter.

Ideally, you will consistently show up as an *Energy Creator,* one who knows how to support and maintain your energy levels to maximize your impact. *Energy Creators* engage fully in the art of living.

Energy Creators tune in and turn on the three P's, characteristics that enable high achievers to function at their full capacity.

Let's get started by exploring the three P's: *Perceptive, Proactive and Purposeful.*®

The individuals who report to you, as well as the ones who supervise you, reap either positive benefits or negative consequences from the energy you emit in the workplace.

"Vision is the art of seeing what is invisible to others."

– Jonathan Swift

1ˢᵀ P: ENERGY CREATORS ARE *PERCEPTIVE!*

When you utilize your perceptiveness, you know yourself and how you relate to and affect others. You see with clarity. You operate in the present moment and tune in to both your observations and your intuitions. You practice mindfulness. You keep your focus primarily on your behavior, rather than on others.

When we get overly focused on those around us, it's critical to notice — as if a "flashing yellow light" were alerting us to potential danger. Our tendency to focus on *external* people or situations can inform us of an *internal* need to address. Often, it's a message that we need to stop and engage in intentional self-care, times of respite, renewal and replenishment from the chronic overload of stressors we carry.

When I find myself criticizing, judging or blaming others, I take a "time out" to get realigned. I recognize that it's time to refocus attention on me.

When I find myself criticizing, judging or blaming others, I take a "time out" to get realigned. I recognize that it's time to refocus attention on me. I know that I will move forward only when I turn the "spotlight" on me.

Taking a break allows me to discern how I can better manage my unmet needs. Ultimately, this allows me to effectively nurture myself so that I may offer presence, compassion and encouragement in my relationships with others as well. When we appreciate and nourish ourselves, we work more collaboratively in the workplace, with our families and throughout our larger communities.

When you are able to see and assess accurately — both internally and externally — while fully aware and awake, you can then be *proactive.*

"The purpose of life is to live it, to taste experience to the utmost, to reach out eagerly and without fear for newer and richer experience."

– Eleanor Roosevelt

2ND P: ENERGY CREATORS ARE *PROACTIVE*!

When you engage proactively, you take decisive action. You see yourself as responsible and capable. You avoid complaining and blaming. You dynamically create options to meet the demands of the particular circumstance you encounter.

Even though you embrace a proactive approach, you may confront situations where you are required to make choices among unwelcome or unpleasant alternatives. However, you can pause to discern the best options, gain clarity and move forward. As you navigate difficult decisions, you build resilience and demonstrate the courage to lead during tumultuous circumstances.

Donna Mack, a treasured friend and colleague from the North Texas chapter of the National Speakers' Association (NSA), described to me how she created an audaciously proactive approach to elevate her speaking career. Once she saw the invitation to submit a proposal to participate in an innovative and difficult format for the 2018 NSA Winter Conference in Baltimore, she fully invested her efforts to be selected to share her wisdom and insights on the main stage.

The guidelines for the five-minute proposed talk would seem daunting for most of us who speak for a living. For Donna, a woman who is blind and utilizes a guide dog, the prospect of beginning a speech in the dark on a platform, with 20 slides advancing automatically every 15 seconds, might have seemed unmanageable. "What if I get behind or can't hear the subtle beeps, my cues to advance the slide?" Donna wondered. Ultimately, she pushed through every form of resistance that arose.

Donna created a two-minute video in her dining room and a proposed topic summary, highlighting what she would explore to illuminate the future of speaking. Before she knew it, she had been selected and went on to deliver a stellar performance. As the saying goes, the rest will be history. Donna's presentation caught fire and immediately propelled her in directions she could hardly imagine a year ago.

When you are fully committed and functional in the moment, you move with *purpose*.

"Happiness is when what you think, what you say, and what you do are in harmony."

– Mahatma Gandhi

As you navigate difficult decisions, you build resilience and demonstrate the courage to lead during tumultuous circumstances.

3ᴿᴰ P: ENERGY CREATORS ARE *PURPOSEFUL!*

As a purposeful creator, you continually advance toward your goals with focus and intention. You clearly understand and define your priorities by what brings you satisfaction and meaning. You remain aware of your inner experience, and use your intuition as a gauge for your strategic moves.

Further, you utilize your insights and actions to stay aligned with your highest priorities and values. You stand unwilling to compromise on your most deeply held beliefs. Importantly, you nurture yourself in a way that allows you to function at optimal capacity the majority of the time.

Let me share a story about an *Energy Creator* who has become one of my favorite sources of inspiration. Dr. John Goodenough, a faculty member at the University of Texas at Austin, eagerly makes his way to work each weekday, as he has for more than three decades.

Okay, you may be wondering, "What's the big deal?" Listen to this! Dr. John's date of birth: July 25, 1922. Not quick with calculations? I'll make it easy for you. As of the publication of this book, Dr. John is close to turning 96 years old.

Dr. John has already made a revolutionary impact on your life by his prolific number of inventions, including the lithium-ion battery. Think: cell phones, computers and defibrillators, all significant to our lives, right? More recently, Dr. John led a team of researchers to submit a patent for a battery that likely will revolutionize electric cars.

Back in his younger days, when he was 30 years old, Dr. John's academic advisor told him that he already had passed the prime age for physicists. Then he suggested that Dr. John should pursue another degree program rather than physics! Thankfully, he was NOT dissuaded from pursuing his dream.

Dr. John thrives on research and new opportunities to improve our world. He continues to work because he recognizes that he has more to accomplish and contribute. What an attitude! His colleagues have described him as the kindest person they know.

Dr. John says, "I'm old enough to know you can't close your mind to new ideas!" How does your thinking compare to this *Energy Creator?*

To come alive and to stay alive, engage your three P's! Be perceptive. Be proactive. Be purposeful.

**To come alive and to stay alive, engage your 3 P's!
Be perceptive. Be proactive. Be purposeful.**

---

* * *

COLLABORATIVE ENERGY

When we engage with others who take full advantage of the three P's, we gain lift from the enhanced momentum, similar to the way a goose creates uplift for the bird immediately following it. By flying in "V" formation, the whole flock improves its flying range 71% more than if each bird flew on its own. People who share a common direction and sense of purpose navigate more quickly and easily because they are traveling on the thrust of one another.

When we operate in an environment that supports our ideas, fuels our creativity and provides us with the tools we need to achieve our goals, our accomplishments are accelerated and limited only by our imaginations. Leaders and managers can cultivate thriving communities within their organizations.

ENERGY MANAGEMENT OR TIME MANAGEMENT?

How can energy management accelerate your success differently than time management? Time management offers you systems to plan how much time you spend on the activities on your to-do list. Implementing this strategy ensures that you get your most important work tasks completed first. Time management supports the process of planning and exercising conscious control of time invested, with efficiency as a desired outcome.

Knowing how to prioritize and structure your work tasks may help you eliminate "work clutter," but you still may not be taking advantage of pivotal times when you operate with optimal energy. We vary in our effectiveness to concentrate and contribute to various tasks throughout the day. We each have our unique times when we work with more lucidity, creativity and clarity, maximizing our output. When we effectively tap into our energy, we often report being "in the flow!"

We simply don't all perform well early in the morning, a common expectation in my previous work life. As a single mother with two young children, I often felt overwhelmed by the task of getting us dressed and fed, with various bags, lunches and necessities, then scurrying out the door to school. Then, I needed to exercise tenacity to make the 45-minute commute to work. I often felt frazzled before my workday began.

One boss (without children) anticipated that I would arrive at my office early, and be clear, focused and ready to produce complex, analytical reports and results. I could pull it off at times, but not routinely. In contrast to her, my most productive times — when truly in the flow of writing, researching, and creating — tended to be in the late morning, afternoon and evening.

We often expend valuable energy trying to generate output when we have yet to warm up. Our production likely will be far more impressive if we tackle our most important tasks during our most alert and free-flowing energy periods.

ENERGY DEPLETORS

You probably know people who slink, slump or skulk into your personal space. You back away from them because you don't sense a positive vibe. You definitely do not want to *be* the person who emits a sense of hopelessness, powerlessness or a "no-way" attitude.

Energy depletors project moods and mindsets that significantly influence the attitudes and outcomes of others in the workplace. You derive benefits from limiting the effect of those who participate in "*impossibility*" rather than "*possibility*" thinking. Maybe you see energy depletors on your work team, in your family or, perhaps, you've even dabbled in impossibility thinking yourself.

Initially we want to offer compassion and kindness to others who are hurting, as evidenced by their negative self-talk, low self-esteem or judgmental attitudes. However, energy depletors must be willing and motivated to release their unhealthy patterns of relating to self and others as well.

Energy depletors often suffer from unrelenting anxiety, tension and burnout from the persistent urgency with which they've pursued their goals. How many of us ignore our personal needs for balance, restoration and self-compassion?

We often lose sight of the high cost of our inattention to and neglect of our requisites for rest and replenishment. A lack of self-care can also result in system breakdowns. Well-timed maintenance and tune-ups work similarly to provide upkeep for our vehicles. Self-nurturing keeps us running smoother, longer and with fewer repair bills. Most visits to our healthcare provider's office result from the chaos and stress we create in our lives.

Energy depletors may benefit from counseling or additional training to learn how to incorporate positive psychology techniques or to develop a more balanced worldview. They most assuredly need to engage in the process of healing those repetitive cycles of negativity. Remember that negative energy, like positive energy, spreads contagiously.

Most visits to our healthcare provider's office result from the chaos and stress we create in our lives.

SELF-CARE STRATEGIES TO RESTORE YOUR ENERGY

Wellness experts, life coaches and physicians emphasize the value that regular self-care activities provide for our overall health and wellness outcomes. Hiatuses from chronic stressors (and from a general state of being overwhelmed) help us to maximize our physical, intellectual, social, spiritual and emotional resources. We increase our likelihood of creating success and happiness in all facets of our lives.

We can dramatically enhance our clarity and creative problem-solving ability when we say yes to intentional self-care, or planned reprieves from daily hassles. When stress and anxiety "take us away," we lose concentration, connection and opportunities to accurately tune in to what's happening in the present.

When we consistently nurture ourselves, we avoid burnout, ethical potholes, and toxic outbursts that characterize those who don't pay attention to their own needs.

Strategic self-care and self-compassion make leaders more resilient, empathic and likeable. When we consistently nurture ourselves, we avoid burnout, ethical potholes, and toxic outbursts that characterize those who don't pay attention to their own needs.

Self-care works best when it is deeply rooted as a reliable way of living and being. When self-care becomes inherent, we engage in self-care continually without having to stop and make a conscious choice. At that point, we have reestablished our way of relating to self and the world.

Energy Creators recognize the importance of building recovery time into their routines. Without sufficient rest, renewal and rejuvenation time, one's concentration, performance and attitude suffer. Although we often hear internalized and popularized messages about pushing through physical and mental limitations to achieve more, we have to take the time to recharge — not endure — to avoid burnout on the various dimensions of wellness.

Mindfulness allows us to be attentive and aware, in the moment, regardless of what's occurring. Mindfulness activities quiet the corrosive chatter, or negative self-talk rant, in which most of us engage.

Ultimately, mindfulness practices support our skills to effectively lead, make wise decisions and navigate work and life stressors. The less well-balanced leaders remain out of touch and ill-prepared to encourage others or to excel, whether in stable work environments or in times of crisis. Ideally, mindfulness practices occur throughout the day, every day.

"People need meaning, vision, purpose and rich relationships."

– Annie McKee

If you want to hire and retain the best workers, those highly committed and talented people who excel as *Energy Creators*, you will succeed if you establish an atmosphere where they:

1. Can envision a meaningful path ahead;
2. Feel connected to a sense of purpose that uplifts both their lives and others; and
3. Establish supportive relationships with managers, colleagues and employees.

Finally, if I've learned anything from the unsettling flurry of funerals and memorial services that I've attended in 2018, it's that people don't give or receive enough positive feedback and loving expressions of kindness.

When we offer caring leadership and a collaborative spirit, no matter where we are in the moment, our world becomes more beautiful.

At the core of our being, we have a deep yearning to know that *who we are* and *what we do* matters to our world. Each of my friends who passed recently deeply touched countless lives. I feel grateful for the powerful wisdom and love that they offered to me. I genuinely hope that they knew how many lives were better because of their presence.

As leaders, we have limitless opportunities to convey empathy, appreciation and kindheartedness. When you do, you foster meaning in people's lives. You also set the wheels in motion to activate even more of the innate talents, abilities and characteristics that lie untapped below the surface.

When we offer caring leadership and a collaborative spirit, no matter where we are in the moment, our world becomes more beautiful. We come alive and thrive with the zeal of an *Energy Creator*!

FOR ONGOING REFLECTION

I'd like to leave you with five questions that I believe can change your life and your career, and that can have remarkable impact on the people around you as well. Go ahead — ask yourself these questions, then get busy being an Energy Creator.

1. How do others react when I enter a room? What do I "*pack along*" that I pass along, whether I intend to or not?

2. How could I shift my energy and positively influence others with whom I connect?

3. What keeps me from recharging when I am feeling depleted?

4. If I really loved and appreciated myself, what would I add or subtract from my life?

5. What's my next step to living as a fully alive *ENERGY CREATOR?*

ABOUT THE AUTHOR

Nancy Little, PhD
LPC, LUT

Dr. Nancy Little enjoyed more than 25 years in higher education and made a significant impact, earning a commendation from the Texas State Senate when she departed from the University of North Texas (UNT) to pursue new opportunities. Nancy envisioned her role as supporting others to achieve their dreams. Whether developing a new campus, writing grants, serving as a trained mediator and diversity leader, teaching master's level counseling courses, offering HR workshops or supporting at-risk students, Nancy excelled due to her deep connection with others.

Today, Nancy is the CEO of Energy Creators®, where she works with organizations and leaders in developing effective energy management strategies. As a heart-opening professional speaker, she encourages audiences with her sensitivity to universal human needs while celebrating individual uniqueness and igniting transformative changes. Nancy achieved professional membership in the National Speakers Association (NSA) in 2015. She serves on the board of NSA North Texas and holds membership in NSA KY and the National Association of Women Business Owners.

A Licensed Professional Counselor (LPC) since 1983, Nancy counseled thousands of clients in her part-time private practice. She supported their emotional health as they explored issues on varied relationship, life change and work-related themes.

She holds a BS in Business Education from the University of Kentucky, an MS in Educational Psychology and Counseling from the University of Kentucky, and a PhD in Counseling with a minor in Psychology from the University of North Texas.

Nancy teaches courses for the UNT Osher Lifelong Learning Institute and serves as an adjunct instructor and subject matter expert on self-care for Unity Worldwide Spiritual Institute. She also consults for Balancing Life's Issues, Inc.

Additionally, Nancy actively participates in Leadership Women. She participated in Leadership Texas ('03), Leadership America ('04) and Leadership International ('13 and '18).

Nancy travels between homes in Flower Mound, TX, and Lexington, KY. She enjoys University of Kentucky college athletics, her role on the Leadership Council for UK Women and Philanthropy, cuddling with her three cats, and exploring with her rescue dog, Lexi, who she adopted with her husband, Russ, in April 2017.

Learn more and contact Nancy:

theenergycreators.com
DrNancyLittle@att.net
Facebook.com/nmlittle1
Twitter.com/drnancylittle
LinkedIn.com/in/nancy-little-phd-lpc-02617716
972-983-3033

Chapter Eleven

KARL RICHTER

"Infovores at Work – How Your Brain Feeds on New Information"

I like to think of myself as a chef. The truth is, I'm a terrible cook and rarely even try something more complicated than a box of mac and cheese. I definitely don't work in a restaurant. I'm a Blended Learning designer.

I started a company called eLearning Blends more than 15 years ago. I work with a team of instructional designers, technology geeks and eLearning developers. I bring the mindset of a chef to the job because we're in charge of feeding the brains of the companies that hire us.

Life in the information age is a steady diet of news feeds and bite-sized updates. We feed on information constantly. For many of us, the internet and smartphones are as vital to our happiness and survival as food and water. These new tools have made our brains evolve into something new. Many of us have become Infovores.

In this chapter, we'll look into the Infovore phenomenon and explore how it impacts you — at work and in your personal life. How do you manage to digest all that information? What's happening in your head when you learn? In this era of over-stimulation, what can you do to be the most effective "You" at Work?

For answers, we'll turn to Cognitive Load theory, the model that researchers use to explain how we process information. You'll learn how your brain is better than a computer, and how Jennifer Aniston helped neuroscientists detect the physical changes that take place in our brain when we learn. Learning takes place inside our heads, but that doesn't mean it's invisible.

How do you manage to digest all that information? What's happening in your head when you learn? In this era of over-stimulation, what can you do to be the most effective "You" at Work?

WHAT IS AN INFOVORE?

"Infovore" has been used by researchers and marketers for more than a decade. Sadly, it isn't a part of mainstream discussion about how our tools have changed us. There are dramatic changes happening to society and we lack the vocabulary to discuss them. I fell in love with the term Infovore at first sight.

My undergrad degree is in anthropology. It's always been a lens I use to view the world. From the anthropologist's point of view, hunting and gathering information is a primal urge. Our instincts give us the hunger for food, the drive to reproduce and the need for a roof over our heads, but smarts are just as important to our survival.

An Infovore feeds on information the way a carnivore eats meat. Our brains have grown used to a steady stream of food-for-thought rushing through our lives. We slurp, sip and gulp down data. It's something we're increasingly dependent upon.

How long can you go without a smartphone? I can't go more than a few hours. I'm an Infovore. These days we rely on the internet and social media the way an herbivore depends on vegetables.

We feed on status updates from our Facebook friends. We digest online articles, blogs and newsletters about our favorite topics. We snack on bites of information whenever we get the chance. Cravings for information can be overpowering. Am I the only one who's ever picked up their smartphone while driving … even though I know it's dumb?

An Infovore feeds on information the way a carnivore eats meat. Our brains have grown used to a steady stream of food-for-thought rushing through our lives.

ARE YOU AN INFOVORE?

If you're reading a chapter of an HR anthology, let's face it, you are. You're more likely to go by the term Lifelong Learner or Knowledge Worker, but you're what others would call an Infovore. You have a magical glass screen in your pocket that you can poke, tap and swipe to access the internet whenever you want from wherever you are. You use it constantly at work and in your personal life.

You're also connected to work every hour of the day. Your Outlook inbox fills up around the clock with information from your colleagues, clients and customers. Notifications blip, bloop and bleep throughout the day. You process questions, updates and reminders that tell you which meeting to head to next.

HOW DO WE DIGEST THESE BITES OF INFORMATION?

You may have heard at some point that the brain works like the processor and hard drive of a computer. Short-term, or working memory, is like your computer's CPU. Everything in working memory is temporary. It's not stored in the brain. It's like an unsaved document during a power outage. Working memory disappears without a trace unless you put in the work to learn it.

Long-term memory is what you've actually learned. The information stored in your brain is like the data stored on the hard drive. It's there, but unlike all the photos on your computer, the memories fade over time.

The computer metaphor is nice because it's easy to wrap your head around it, but for me it falls flat. The axons and dendrites living at the ends of the neurons in your head are much more exciting than the lifeless hunks of metal, solder and plastic you see at Best Buy.

We are not hard-wired like a laptop from Best Buy. We are capable of powerful change. Our brains are not soldered in place when we reach our adult years. In fact, it's the opposite! We're constantly learning. The brain is constantly rewiring its connections through what researchers call neuroplasticity. We're always learning and our brains are always changing.

THE JENNIFER ANISTON NEURON

Learning takes place inside our skulls, but that doesn't mean the changes are invisible. Dr. John Medina's book, *Brain Rules*, tells the story of the Jennifer Aniston neuron. I think his summary of the research and implications on neuroscience are at least as hot as Rachel Green from "Friends."

Researchers use fMRI and PET scans to detect real, physical changes taking place in our brains when we think and learn. Medina and his team ran an experiment where they scanned a person's brain activity while they showed a number of different pictures, including some including Jennifer Aniston. They discovered a specific neuron that would fire when shown a picture of Jen. These neurons had formed a synapse — a new connection between brain cells. That same neuron would fire for anything Jennifer Aniston. It fired when presented with pictures of her and her famous haircut from early seasons of "Friends," through the Brad Pitt years and into today.

Remarkably, the neuron would not fire when shown different pictures. It wouldn't light up for photos of Christina Applegate or Kristen Wiig. It wouldn't light up in someone who was trapped under a rock for 20 years and had never heard of the famous actress. The neuron only lights up for someone who had been exposed to Jennifer Aniston and knew her work.

This is significant because researchers found physical evidence that the brain's structure had adapted to the idea of Jennifer Aniston. Our brains are complex and there's so much we don't know. This discovery is like finding a needle in a haystack. It gave us tangible proof that our brains adapt to the information we feed them and that learning changes our brain.

As we learn, we form new synapses or connections between neurons. Each neuron has dendrites that bring information to the cell and axons that pass it on to a dendrite of a nearby brain cell. Over time, those neurons are coated in a fatty white covering called myelin. The thicker the coating around those brain cells, the more experience a person has with a given subject.

Experts are able to recall the information more quickly with less effort because the neurons have a sheath of myelin, which helps them fire and call upon information more quickly.

BRIDGING THE GAP

If it helps, think of building the neural synapse like building a special kind of rope bridge.[1] In this metaphor, you're a bit like a spider trying to connect two sides of a river. Think of how a spider builds a web. As it moves, it leaves a strand behind it. Imagine that each time you cross the bridge, you lay down a new strand of rope. As you think about a topic, the synapse fires and the connection between the cells gets stronger. With each trip across

---

1   The rope bridge metaphor isn't perfect either. Brain cells don't actually physically connect, but the synapse between them strengthens and gets more efficient each time we fire the brain. The more a synapse fires, the more myelin lines the brain cells involved.

the synapse, the rope bridge slowly turns from a tightrope into a stable suspension bridge.

The bridges you cross regularly become tasks you can do on auto-pilot. Can you write your name without much effort? Sure, but you couldn't when you were four years old. When learning a new task, you'll be slower and less confident until you practice. You'll use more effort until the cells in that synapse have more myelin.

YOUR BRAIN IS BETTER THAN A COMPUTER

A laptop doesn't adapt to expertise. It never starts processing information faster, but we do! That's why the brain-as-computer metaphor leaves out my favorite part of the job: helping people perform. I'm in the business of cooking up ways for employees to build skills. With enough practice, you build automaticity and you do it effortlessly. Your laptop doesn't get faster over time. In fact, it'll never be as fast as the first day you have it.

I'm in the business of cooking up ways for employees to build skills. With enough practice, you build automaticity and you do it effortlessly.

I like the rest of the computer metaphor. Evidence from research shows that we process information in working memory. Working memory is actually divided into two channels. The first is what we hear, the second channel is what see. The audio and visual channels of our working memory work together to help us process the world around us.

Learning is all about taking information from working memory and encoding it into the synapses in our long-term memory. We physically build structures in our brain as we learn. That's why I like to think of myself as a chef. I am trying to nourish your brain and help it grow new synapses.

As a parent, I try to get our four preschool boys to eat nutritious meals. (Or at least mac and cheese.) It can be tricky to find a balance between what's yummy and what's good for you. As a learning designer, I try to find the sweet spot between interesting and informative. A dull eLearning module isn't memorable. It may be accurate, but it's not likely to have much of an impact unless learners engage with it. If their neurons aren't firing as they take it, it won't strengthen the synapses in their brains. It's like a pile of spinach left untouched on the plate.

I'm a Blended Learning Specialist because I believe in the neuroscience behind it. I feel like a chef because our goal is to nourish the specific skills your organization needs. I help my clients use a wide range of different technologies to engage learners and build those synapses over time. We don't just build online modules, job aids or face-to-face exercises. We blend these and other solutions together in a custom recipe for you.

When I *do* cook, I'm the kind of chef who likes everyone to be able to take home leftovers. Here are five of my favorite tips for success based on Cognitive Load Theory. I hope you can take at least one of them home with you.

Tip 1. Blend Technologies

I make online modules, but never encourage my clients to remove all face-to-face training. Instead, I suggest you take advantage of the strengths and weaknesses of each. There's a magic sparked by people in a room that online learning can never create. On the other hand, self-study modules are much more flexible and efficient. Use both. Don't have the sales team fly in for two days of lectures! Even Infovores can't drink from a fire hose. Give them lectures as short videos that are pre-work. Then, when they're together in the room let facilitators fire up the troops (and their neurons) during participant-centered learning.

Close your door and think. Sit still without guilt. You're hard at work! Learning is a physical change happening in your brain; you need to give it time to create the connection.

Tip 2. Stop and Think

Keep sanity a part of your personal and professional lives. There's a neurological need for five seconds of reflection throughout the day. Five minutes is even better. As you think through an issue, you're building the synapses your brain needs to learn.

Close your door and think. Sit still without guilt. You're hard at work! Learning is a physical change happening in your brain; you need to give it time to create the connection.

Tip 3. Work Out

You wouldn't expect to get in shape by going for one jog. Learning doesn't work that way either. You need to flex your mental muscles consistently to fire the neurons that support the skills you need at work.

Don't look at journaling, debriefing a meeting with a colleague, or reviewing your notes as a waste of time. They're a critical part of what makes your brain a success at work. These activities are your brain's opportunity to encode working memory into permanent and lasting long-term memory. The act of firing those neurons is what it takes to change your brain.

Tip 4. Prioritize

Preserve your cognitive resources. I joke that your brain is on a fixed income. There's only so much it can pay attention to.

Prioritize what you can look up in time of need versus what you need to put in the work to memorize. Your brain can't learn it all. Our information-age tools give us access to information more efficiently than ever. Don't be afraid to look it up. Work smart, not hard.

Tip 5. Reduce, Reuse, Recycle

To communicate more clearly, avoid the information dump. Instead, use what they already know and build on that. We all have a finite amount of working memory. Accept those limitations and plan accordingly.

If you're making a presentation, give your audience time for Q&A throughout a presentation, not just on the very last slide. The time they spend actively thinking and asking questions gives brains the opportunity to move info from working memory to long-term memory. The wheels need to turn to encode new information. Cognitively speaking, discussion isn't inefficient, skipping it is.

If you prefer more structure, stop throughout the presentation and ask them questions that will help them integrate what you're telling them with what they already know. Instead of dumping new information on them, recycle and reuse what they already know with a mix of new information you're giving them.

PARTING THOUGHTS

The world has changed tremendously since the rise of the World Wide Web. The amount of information in the universe continues to expand while our attention spans continue to shrink. Our appetite for information has grown. We feed our brains with the information we need to survive at work and in our social circles. We've evolved into Infovores who crave new information constantly.

Our brains have done a wonderful job adapting to the changing times, but for the most effective You at Work, don't overload your Working Memory; take mindful steps to make it work for you.

ABOUT THE AUTHOR

Karl Richter
MA, Educational Technology

Karl Richter is the Owner and Creative Director at eLearning Blends, an instructional design company that specializes in Blended Learning. His team creates custom eLearning that integrates with classroom experiences, coaching and performance support tools. Karl is an eLearning Coach. He works on site or online with organizations looking to raise the bar for engaging and effective training programs. He facilitates workshops on popular topics like brain-based instructional design, blended learning, and hands-on software training using tools like Articulate Storyline.

Karl is also a writer who is hopelessly addicted to puns and wordplay. His site, eLearningRecipes.com , uses a fun series of food metaphors to help learning designers find mouth-watering combinations of different learning technologies. Recipes list different technologies like the ingredients in a meal. They provide step-by-step directions for how to cook one up on your own.

Karl is highly regarded for his expertise in helping companies leverage technology to train their people affordably and efficiently. He's a firm believer that the best training is not only accurate, but memorable enough to change behavior. His speaking style is humorous, well-researched and practical.

Karl earned his MA in Educational Technology from San Diego State University in 2006 where he was an online and campus instructor in the Educational Technology Department through 2010. He also holds a BA in Linguistics and Anthropology from the University of Southern California.

Karl lives in Louisville, Kentucky, with his beautiful wife, four boys and a dog named Derby.

Learn more and contact Karl:

Elearningblends.com

Karl@elearningblends.com

Linkedin.com/in/elearningblends

Twitter.com/elearningblends

Youtube.com/user/eLearningBlends

Chapter Twelve

LISA SEAY

"I'm the Boss ... Now What? Moving from Threatened to Thrilled to Thriving"

As an HR leader, I've seen it time and time again: Great employees who aspire to leadership. Yet, once they achieve it, they become disenfranchised and wonder why they ever wished for it. Or, those who become a leader simply because it's the next natural step (or possibly the only way to earn more money). However, after arriving in their new role, they are thrust into unknown territory without the necessary support to thrive. These leaders who were bright-eyed and ready to change the world now question their own abilities, experience extreme highs and lows, and often mistake the resulting missteps, self-doubt and general anxiety to mean that they're just not cut out to be a leader.

How do I know this? Because I've experienced it.

"Be careful what you wish for," I told myself not long after being given what could only be considered good news concerning my own path to leadership. It was early in my career and I was loving my role in the healthcare industry. One day, I spoke up to my boss and said, "I want to learn more and do more ... just so you know." Well, it wasn't too long after that when I found myself as the leader of a team of three, overseeing work I had not specifically done myself and wondering exactly what I had wished for.

It was the best and worst of times. Really. I couldn't believe I'd received this opportunity to lead Human Resources in the second largest division of the company, which coincidentally had just been acquired. Talk about the blind leading the blind! A lot can be learned when you have no choice but to jump in. Fast forward 15 years later. I've had more opportunities to lead, to be led and to support leaders. One thing I know for sure … our world needs leaders — and not just the kind who have a title, and if they're lucky, a parking spot and a corner office. This world needs people at all levels, in all environments — business and otherwise — who walk the talk, show the way and create the change needed for our future.

Yet, there are many, like me, who find themselves in leadership, excited about the opportunity but who have no real experience or background to support them in getting off to a productive and meaningful start. Or possibly, they've convinced themselves they don't have the background to be a successful leader. Soon, the excitement experienced after hearing of one's promotion quickly turns into feeling unsure and ill-equipped … essentially, threatened.

When the brain senses threat, it triggers neurophysiological activity that reorganizes the brain's resources and attention so that it can focus on keeping you safe. Didn't realize all of that was happening in your body, all the while you're trying to do your job? When we're trying to protect ourselves from a perceived threat, it's pretty hard to *thrive* at the same time.

OLD VERSUS NEW LEADERSHIP

In the 2017 Deloitte Global Human Capital Trends report,[1] a comparison is made between the old rules of leadership vs. the new rules we see in play today. Old rules, according to the report, stated that leaders must "pay their dues" to work their way up the leadership pipeline. The new rule is that leaders are identified early and given "early, outsized responsibility to test and develop their leadership skills." Once upon a time, leaders were identified and assessed based on past experience, tenure and business performance. Now, leaders are assessed early in their careers for agility, creativity and the ability to lead and connect teams (often when they've never formally done it before). Traditionally, leaders were expected to know what to do and expected to bring judgment and experience to new business challenges. Today, experience is not necessarily king. Instead, leaders are expected to innovate, collaborate and to work through teams to find new solutions.

Once upon a time, leaders were identified and assessed based on past experience, tenure and business performance. Now, leaders are assessed early in their careers for agility, creativity and the ability to lead and connect teams (often when they've never formally done it before).

Interestingly enough, developing existing leaders as well as future leaders requires us to consider not only what workplaces look like now, but what we expect them to look like in years to come. Deloitte asserts,

---

1   *Rewriting the Rules for the Digital Age: 2017 Deloitte Global Human Capital Trends*, https://www2.deloitte.com/content/dam/Deloitte/global/Documents/About-Deloitte/central-europe/ce-global-human-capital-trends.pdf

"High-performing leaders today need different skills and expertise than in generations past, yet most organizations have not moved rapidly enough to develop digital leaders, promote young leaders and build new leadership models." They go on to say that a new type of leader is needed: One who must "understand how to build and lead teams; keep people connected and engaged; and drive a culture of innovation, learning and continuous improvement. They must also be able to lead a workforce that now includes contractors — the contingent workforce — and crowd talent."

No small undertaking, to be sure.

In my experience supporting and coaching leaders, I've seen some common areas in which they struggle. Perhaps I've been particularly attuned because I've had the same struggles. It's important to recognize these struggles so that instead of fearing or resisting them, we can utilize them as a part of our development.

COMMON STRUGGLES FOR NEW LEADERS

While I'm taking time to highlight a few common struggles new leaders often face, I'm not suggesting that, by knowing these or understanding them from a theoretical point of view, it's advisable or even possible to avoid these struggles altogether: It is through the struggle that true growth takes place. So, recognize the struggle, welcome it and even sit with it awhile. Instead of beating yourself up as you go through it or thinking that in some way, you should be above it, embrace the struggle for all that it will provide to you as a developing leader. After all, aren't we all developing in one way or another? I, for one, certainly hope so because the alternative is a life of limited thinking, limited being and, ultimately, limited growth.

Side note: If you're a relatively experienced leader reading this, consider reaching out to the less-experienced leaders around you. Whether they're in the workplace, in your community, your professional organizations or volunteer groups, leaders and potential leaders are all around us. It is the responsibility of those who have weathered a few more storms and endured a few battles to teach, mentor and guide those who are just beginning. Remember that as you support others in their leadership journey, you are helping to shape and inspire those who can lead proactively and constructively in the future. And, that's good for all of us.

As you support others in their leadership journey, you are helping to shape and inspire those who can lead proactively and constructively in the future. And, that's good for all of us.

Let's jump in.

Struggle #1: You continue acting as you did before you became the leader.

When taking on a leadership role, particularly in an organization where you've already been a team member, it can be a difficult transition to move away from the "doing" to the "leading." So, you keep doing your old job. There are a number of reasons why this could happen. Sometimes there's no one else to take over the responsibilities you had under your previous role. Or maybe your internal and external customers just can't adjust to working with someone else — after all, you know them and it's just a quick question they have for you. Another more subtle reason that new leaders keep doing their old jobs is that it's comfortable and they're good at it; they're not yet accomplished in their new role, so it's more satisfying to do the role they know. While all these reasons are understandable, you aren't doing yourself a favor by continuing to perform at a team member level and not rising to the occasion to provide direction and oversight. It doesn't serve your team, and ultimately won't serve you to avoid establishing yourself as the leader.

Struggle #2: You're unsure how to establish relationships with your team.

Perhaps you've been a part of the team and now you're the boss. Or, you're joining a new organization in a leadership role where one of the team members you're leading wanted the job and you were chosen instead. Your calendar is starting to fill up with all the meetings you have to attend because now … you're in leadership. And, there are more systems to learn, reports to complete and people to meet. Often, new leaders don't spend the time really getting to know their teams because they're consumed with the pomp and circumstance of their new role. Or, they have a hard time making the transition from "one of the gang" to the leader of the pack.

Often, new leaders don't spend the time really getting to know their teams because they're consumed with the pomp and circumstance of their new role. Or, they have a hard time making the transition from "one of the gang" to the leader of the pack.

Don't miss the opportunity to learn from your team. Get to know them and find out how you can support them, even if you think you already know what they know or what support they need. Dr. Stephen R. Covey wrote about the emotional bank account where all interactions in our relationships result in an increase or decrease in the balance of trust and connection. According to his theory, all the touchpoints we have with our team have the ability to increase or decrease the trust account. Every activity (no matter how big or small) is a deposit into or withdrawal from the "trust" bank, and a healthy trust bank will be the foundation of a high-performing team.

Struggle #3: You're inexperienced in managing up.

Your leadership role requires that you not only effectively lead your team but that you also make sure that those above you and next to you — your peers — have the information, updates and input from your team for them to do their jobs and feel confident that you and your team are doing yours. It's a tall order, no doubt. Navigating internal politics that may exist in an organization often catches new leaders by surprise. Having often been shielded from such things in the past, new leaders may be completely unaware of the importance of these relationships and the appropriate way to build and mange them.

A lot of useful information exists to guide you, particularly in the area of managing your boss.[2] For starters, even if you don't like or respect each other, it's still important to anticipate your boss's needs, disagree respectfully and perhaps most importantly, be a source of help. Managing up is not about a popularity contest or making sure you don't rock the boat. It's about leveraging your position and partnering with those below you and those above you to perform at the highest level possible.

---

2   For more information about managing your boss, I suggest checking out this *Harvard Business Review* article by Dana Rousmaniere: https://hbr.org/2015/01/what-everyone-should-know-about-managing-up.

NOW WHAT?

As you can imagine, coming up against even one of these three struggles can cause a new leader to feel inadequate, judged, demoralized and just plain unfit for the position they so eagerly sought and were chosen for because of superb past performance.

But, the story can't end there. If leaders throw in the towel, decide it's just too hard, want to go back to the safety and security of not being in front, what happens to our world? We need leaders in both informal and formal roles who can influence and impact not only our workplaces, but our classrooms, communities, civic groups and the world at large.

MOVING FROM THREATENING TO THRILLING TO THRIVING

If you are a roller coaster enthusiast, you may particularly understand why rides that make you scream and *slightly* make you fear for your life are so attractive. Researcher Malcom Burt has studied this and found that waiting in line for that famous coaster is more frightening to people than the actual ride. He said, in reference to going on a famous roller coaster called The Giant Drop, "I honestly feel like I'm going to cry, but I do it and what an incredible feeling you get when you get off."[3]

Can the same be said of leadership? Is there more fear in the anticipation of the role than the actual ride itself?

---

3   Leanne Edmistone, "Thrill Seeker," U on Sunday, *The Courier Mail*, Feb. 22, 2105, https://static1.squarespace.com/static/547befffe4b07347e774e29e/t/5a830340652de-a92b60b581e/1518535499639/0011.+Dare.pdf.

You *can* move from the thrill of your new leadership position to thriving in it. You may take a step or two forward and then slide back. But, continue to embrace the struggles, examine the source of your fear and enlist the support you need. Like anything new, anticipate a period of trial and error. Success takes practice and repetition. As you encounter the struggles and think about how to respond, consider the following suggestions:

Ask for the help you need.

Simple to say but hard to do. After all, weren't you promoted because you know everything already? Not really! In fact, in the story of my promotion into the role I wanted but wasn't sure I was ready for, my boss told me the main reason I was promoted was that they trusted me and knew I would ask questions about the things I didn't know.

If you wait for others to come to you to provide you with training or to answer the questions that they think you might have, you will be waiting for a while.

Simply stated: If you wait for others to come to you to provide you with training or to answer the questions that they think you *might* have, you will be waiting for a while.

In the Deloitte study cited earlier in this chapter, the authors maintain that more than 44 percent of Millennials are now in leadership positions, but most believe they are receiving little to no development in their roles. Yet 54 percent of companies report they have excellent or adequate programs for Millennials. Clearly, formal programs are only part of the answer and it must be the new leader's responsibility to seek out the help, internally or externally, that they need to thrive in the new position.

Engage in continuous learning.

The constancy of change in our world demands that we are always learning new things. The way things were done yesterday are not how they will be done in the future. Continuous learning can be approached in a variety of ways. Whether it's seeking a new point of view, reading a book on a topic you're dealing with, or having a conversation (not a series of text messages) about how to handle a challenging situation, you can learn something new.

I've also found that the learning may not come exactly when you seek it. Simply because you are advised to pursue a certain path, or you read an article or a book about what someone else has done, doesn't mean that you have *learned*. Your learning will take place through the hard work of *doing*. By engaging in the work, with the people who do the work to obtain the best outcome possible, you cannot help but learn. But, stay diligent. Seek opportunities to do things you haven't done before with people you haven't done them with.

Leave a legacy.

Never forget that your role as a leader, whether or not you're making more money or you have a fancy title, is vital; and you've taken it on for a reason. Step into the challenge, for by doing so, you have the opportunity to make a difference and to leave a legacy. It could be that one day in the far distant future, someone you're interacting with today becomes a better leader because of your example. Or, something is accomplished because of your vision and tenacity to see it through. You may not be recognized for it and you may feel like it's more work than it's worth, but when you believe in something and you believe in the people doing it, it's always worth it.

STEPPING UP TO THAT "I'M THE BOSS" MOMENT

Unless you're about to retire, the time is coming for you — the time when you'll be thrust or invited into a new level of leadership. Are you ready? Whether you feel ready to be the boss or are terrified of the prospect, the opportunities inherent in the experience are endless. Perhaps you'll "win" — you'll be a great leader and you'll enjoy every moment of it. And if you don't have the exact outcome you had hoped for, you'll learn.

By stepping up to lead when the opportunity arises, you seize the chance impact those around you in ways you may never know. More importantly, you'll learn that experiencing the thrill that can come with threat will only serve to help you thrive as a leader, now and in the future.

ABOUT THE AUTHOR

Lisa Seay

MBA, SPHR, ACC

Lisa Seay is on a mission to help individuals find their professional purpose (and power!), and to help companies develop cost-effective, efficient and sustainable talent management strategies. As founder of the coaching/consulting firm element c, Lisa leverages her HR background to provide coaching, leadership development and team building services.

By virtue of having worked in myriad environments during her 25-year corporate career — including Internet startups, mergers and acquisitions, franchised organizations and large entities with multi-state locations — she knows firsthand the degrees to which challenging organizational situations can impact workforce performance, employee engagement and personal career growth.

Prior to launching element c in 2015, Lisa held talent management and HR director roles in a variety of organizations, including A.T. Kearney and Baylor Health Care System. Most recently, she served as a National Director of Human Resources at Conifer Health Solutions in Frisco, Texas, where she led a team that supported 3,000+ employees. During Lisa's tenure at Yum! Brands/Pizza Hut, Inc., she managed a $500K employee marketing initiative that attracted 250,000+ job seekers to the company's new online application system in three months.

A proponent of life-long learning, Lisa holds a Master of Business Administration degree from Southern Methodist University, a Graduate Certificate in Executive Coaching from the University of Texas at Dallas and is an Associate Certified Coach through the International Coach Federation. She also holds a BA in Communication Studies from the University of North Texas.

Lisa lives outside Dallas with her husband, Brian, who works in the financial services industry, and their 12- and 9-year-old daughters. She is the New Family Liaison at her children's school, and serves on the personnel committee at her church. She is incredibly passionate about working with leaders on the struggles and related solutions explored in this book chapter.

Learn more and contact Lisa:

Lisa@theelementc.com

Facebook.com/theelementc

LinkedIn.com/in/seaylisa

theelementc.com

Chapter Thirteen

MICHELE LAWLIS SHELTON

"Dimensionally Yours: A Renewed Pledge to Inclusion"

May your choices reflect your hopes, not your fears.

– Nelson Mandela

Creating a diverse and inclusive culture is NOT an overnight process. The journey can include a series of people and policy changes that, depending upon the goals and commitment of your company or organization, could precede months and even years before a true shift in your workplace culture occurs. Do you ever wonder how it's possible to stay motivated and perform at your peak when your experience consists of the repetitive delivery or hearing of the same message — to or by the same people — while receiving the same result … only a slight move of the needle? If this sounds familiar to you, then you are at the right place, at the right time. *Every* diversity leader/advocate needs to stop and refuel every now and then, so here's your chance.

Over the next few pages, we're going to focus on the organization and you. Yes, *you* the [Position/Title] of [Company or Organization Name]. If you hold any role where you have responsibility for managing or supervising others, you play an integral part in the implementation of the diversity and inclusion strategy, as well as its success in creating a workplace committed to equity, community building, positive human relations and the attainment of all other organizational goals. Please note that you will enjoy this experience more if you embrace the following disclaimer as a prerequisite to the rest of this chapter:

The chief diversity officer, human resources or diversity departments cannot and should not carry the unilateral burden of proof for the advocacy, development and implementation of your inclusion strategy. Their responsibility is to guide you along a hopeful journey.

THE JOURNEY

The journey to inclusion is an ongoing cyclical experience. The first stop on the journey requires courage: the courage to give an honest assessment of the organization's culture relative to promoting and sustaining inclusion. It raises the question of what shapes organizational culture, and what are the knowledge and skills required to promote and sustain inclusion? Answers to the assessment usually reveal an issue that requires immediate attention and leaders are convinced to take action to address that issue. Successful resolution of the issue creates a level of comfort that celebrates the progress until another challenge surfaces, once again requiring an honest assessment of culture.

Organizations determined to attract and retain the best talent, fulfill their mission and maintain a competitive edge, need leaders who can effectively manage human relations in the workplace and influence culture by showing up as authentic, trustworthy and intentional in meeting the needs of both the organization and its internal customers, the employees.

THE CULTURE SHIFT

Organizational leaders no longer control culture. No longer is management charged solely with providing the logistical needs of a safe and secure location, a workspace within that location, adequate tools or supplies, a break room with appliances *and* vending machines, performance expectations, and last but certainly not least, benefits and compensation for the job performed. We have experienced a culture shift wherein today's workforce is looking for an experience ripe with purpose, presence and prioritization. Organizations determined to attract and retain the best talent, fulfill their mission and maintain a competitive edge, need leaders who can effectively manage human relations in the workplace and influence culture by showing up as authentic, trustworthy and intentional in meeting the needs of both the organization and its internal customers, the employees. If I were to give this to you, straight no chaser, it means there are now two bottom lines, and neither will accept second class citizenship.

THE POWER OF HOPE

I started my career in city government as an Equal Employment Opportunity (EEO) compliance officer charged with enforcing Title VII of the Civil Rights Act of 1964 and other employment laws. In that role, I conducted training seminars on employment rights and investigated hundreds of discrimination and sexual harassment cases for corporations. I resolved many cases through mediation or negotiated settlements where thousands of dollars in damages and/or back pay were secured for aggrieved parties. Other cases resulted in a finding of no probable cause, and the parties either separated or continued their employment relationship. However, in every instance, and regardless of the outcome, there was one common occurrence: The hope of sharing a brighter future, together, seemed to dwindle for both the employee and the employer.

In September of 2017 I attended, for the first time, a naturalization ceremony. If you have never done so, I highly recommend it. I was so proud of my country and moved to tears by the enthusiasm and hope displayed in the collective eye of my new American brothers and sisters. I know why I love my country, yet I couldn't help but wonder at that moment what was the "why" for each individual participating in that ceremony. What is it about becoming an American citizen, for them, that caused no fear in entirely renouncing all allegiance and fidelity to their native lands in exchange for a promise of life, liberty and the pursuit of happiness? And then I noticed on the back of the program an explanation that not only answered but silenced my questions forever:

"You who have been born in America,

I wish I could make you understand what it is like

not to be an American;

not to have been an American all your life;

and then suddenly with the words of a man in flowing robes

to be one, for that moment and forever after.

One moment you belong with your fathers;

to a million dead yesterdays;

the next you belong with America

to a million unborn tomorrows."

  – George Magar Mardikian

My new brothers and sisters were eager for the perceived belonging, opportunity and hope that springs eternal for citizens of our country. For someone who desires to move beyond their past, for whatever reason, and look forward to a brighter future America provides a form of hope that sustains life just like the air that we breathe. This hope is stronger than any fear of the unknown, commands full allegiance, an adherence to the laws and a trust that America will keep her promises to all citizens. And when she doesn't, the effect on hope and the human spirit can be devastating.

Many employer/employee relationships carry similar characteristics. The hope and anticipation of receiving a job offer is an emotional rollercoaster ride throughout the application and selection processes, especially in today's job market where so many processes are automated. Receiving an invitation to interview for a position is not always a reflection of your qualifications or ability, but often reflects the outcome of a numbers game wherein your application may have landed, fortunately, within the first stack pulled from the applicant tracking system and reviewed by recruiters. When you receive that first email communication, you hold your breath until you see "Thank you for applying, but we've decided to move forward with other candidates," or "We would like to schedule you for an interview." Upon successful completion of the interview and selection process, the employee life-cycle begins.

Every new hire comes into your organization in transition from "the end" of something (voluntarily or involuntarily) and into a hopeful new beginning. Each employee pledges allegiance to their employers through their commitment to perform and produce according to terms and methods established by the employer. In exchange for their allegiance and choice to bring their knowledge and talents to the organization, the employee trusts the employer to keep its promise of welcoming the employee as a full-fledged citizen of the organization, entitled to the full enjoyment of its culture as expressed through the mission, vision and values. If the culture is not reflective of the promise, and the employee is refused access to any of the rights and privileges of organizational citizenship, once again the effect can be devastating, and the hope of sharing a brighter future can be lost.

THE AMBASSADOR

Leaders within an organization serve not only as authority figures, but as ambassadors of hope, whether they realize it or not. Inclusive leaders see it as a challenge and a privilege to do so, because that hope is realized through fulfillment of the bottom line of each individual employee: A bottom line that is determined by their personal mission, vision and values as influenced by the many dimensions of their upbringing, background and life experiences.

Consider for a moment whether you function as an authority or an ambassador within your organization. As an authority figure, a leader issues demands, evaluates rule adherence and manages productivity. As an ambassador to your workforce, or citizens, your expertise is needed to help employees navigate the unknown terrain of your organization to successfully achieve expectations for both the employer and themselves. There is nothing more frustrating than coming into an organization, not knowing what you don't know, and having a leader who is unwilling to share organizational knowledge, speak up for you by acknowledging your abilities and contributions across the organization, or speak out for you by refusing to allow you to be subjected to organizational injustice.

Leaders within an organization serve not only as authority figures, but as ambassadors of hope, whether they realize it or not.

Employees are becoming less responsive to leaders who rule with an iron fist or display a lack of integrity; instead they are seeking out those who are not afraid of the unknown, social transparency or collaboration. A renewed pledge to inclusion requires organizational leaders to choose to serve as ambassadors in helping their workforce achieve their personal bottom line, while working together to achieve the bottom line of the organization. This expectation openly promotes a camaraderie that is vastly different from the traditional management/workforce relationship, or the "us vs. them" mentality that has existed within the workplace throughout multiple generations.

According to FastCompany.com, millennials will comprise 75% of the workforce by the year 2025. Millennials, on the heels of Baby Boomers and GenXers, will not waste time continuing to "talk" about inclusion; they will pursue workplace environments where inclusion is no longer a buzz word, but the obvious standard within the culture. As the workforce continues to diversify, companies will struggle to retain talent without prioritizing their individual needs as equally important as those of the organization.

Do you recall why you said "yes" to accepting the employment offer from your current employer? Were you just looking for a job or were you inspired by the organizational brand, product, service or values? Let's take a moment to reflect on your initial expectations. Have they all been fulfilled, or do you still have hope that in time you will achieve your goals? If the answer is "yes," then your job as a leader is to ensure the same experience for your workforce. If the answer is "no," then I challenge you to be an advocate for pursuing the changes that are necessary to ensure the answer becomes a "yes" for you and others. It is within these hopes and expectations — or the personal bottom line — where the true motivation for employee engagement and performance are found for both you and your workforce. Remember, we're all in this together.

A NEW ERA

In 2007, I was the keynote speaker at a graduation ceremony for an adult professional development program. As I completed my address on *Preparing for the 21ˢᵗ Century Workplace*, the spouse of one of the graduates came right over to me and said, "Do you have a book? It would really be helpful if I could take a copy of it to the leaders back at my company." I replied, no, and that I was just sharing my thoughts on cultural shifts I anticipated would occur in the workplace based on my work and observations in human relations. He responded, "Well you really should think about putting your thoughts into a book. We're in a new era; employees are different now, and we've been trying to get our leaders to understand this for months. You hit the nail right on the head."

He thanked me once again and then left to rejoin his family. I never saw him again, but his words stayed with me. They stayed because he validated the relevancy and timeliness of my insights, and uncovered another avenue through which I could support others in the pursuit of inclusion. The experience started a new era for me as an author. There are many employees seeking opportunities to maximize their potential. What insights are you holding that could open the door to a new era for your workforce? Let's unlock your potential to unleash them.

Your contribution to the rest of the world is rooted in your **authenticity**. We cannot celebrate what we do not know. It is imperative that inclusion advocates and leaders embrace the diversity that lies within themselves. You are an ever-evolving spirit having a human experience of multiple dimensions. You are comprised of a variety of experiences in and out of your control that have culminated in who you have become personally and professionally. Explore that with the intention of maximizing your strengths, acknowledging your weaknesses, and strengthening your resolve to build bridges with people who can complement you by adding to your knowledge and quality of life.

Your contribution to the rest of the world is rooted in your *authenticity*.

As you gain greater appreciation for those who can bring a different perspective to your life experience, recognize the value in that perspective. Instead of allowing stereotypes and assumptions to create false illusions, honor their journey by extending to them the opportunity to share their truths and show you who they are. Embrace the conviction to act with **integrity** and treat them with fairness and platinum respect always.

The more you are viewed as a leader who is **intentional** about promoting inclusive representation, recognition and collaboration, you will establish a **trust** that opens the door to mutual transparency. On the other side of that transparency, my wish is that you and your employees choose the hope of today over the fears of yesterday to carry you and your organization into many tomorrows together. If you're ready to continue the journey, it's time to take the pledge.

PLEDGE TO INCLUSION

As an inclusion advocate, employee or member of [Insert Name of Company or Organization], I will support its mission to [Insert Company or Organization's Mission] through practicing the values of [Insert Company or Organization's Values].

In honor of our guiding principles, I will:

- ✓ Act intentionally and proactively to champion diversity and inclusion.

- ✓ Encourage open and honest dialogue to enhance communication and build trust.

- ✓ Use a collaborative approach to develop and expand our organization.

- ✓ Focus on delivering innovative approaches, quality products and excellent customer service.

- ✓ Manage all internal and external resources in an efficient, ethical and effective manner.

This I pledge as my ongoing commitment to supporting the continued growth and viability of the business and community climates in [Insert State, Country], and our global society.

A MESSAGE TO MY FELLOW DIVERSITY CHAMPIONS

I celebrate and promote inclusion as a diversity advocate because with all my personal experiences, unique qualities and complexities, I am the manifestation of it, and thankfully so are you. The true reward of diversity is revealed when we discover the heart of another and recognize it as our own.

Until we meet again ... stay strong and be encouraged.

Dimensionally Yours,
Michele Lawlis Shelton

ABOUT THE AUTHOR

Michele Lawlis Shelton

Michele Lawlis Shelton is a speaker, coach and performance consultant on human relations in the workplace. She uses her experience from "both sides of the aisle" as a former equal employment opportunity investigator and human resources executive to provide inclusion solutions that equip public, private and non-profit sector leaders to *transform their work environment into an experience!* Michele has been a highly sought-after presenter for entry-level to C-suite audiences because of her relatability, transparency and candor on the condition of the 21st century workplace.

Michele has more than 15 years of experience designing and leading strategic HR and diversity initiatives that support organizational objectives, meet compliance standards and promote employee engagement. She served previously — by appointment of Kentucky's 61st Governor — as executive director of the Office of Diversity & Equality for the Commonwealth of Kentucky Personnel Cabinet, where she provided visionary leadership to strategically transform the development of policies and practices to advance an EEO, affirmative action and diversity doctrine impacting 33,000+ state employees. Michele also provided leadership to the Personnel Cabinet as director of Strategic Partnerships and Mission Integration, serving as coach and consultant to agency leaders re-aligning their departments to achieve the administration's workforce objectives.

In other leadership roles, Michele has provided oversight to the administration of national workforce development, supplier diversity and women's initiatives. She holds a BA in Political Science from the University of Louisville, a certificate in church studies from Louisville Seminary, and additional graduate study in Human Resources Development at Webster University. She is a member of the Society for Human Resource Management, Association for Talent Development, and National Speakers Association.

Michele lives in her hometown of Louisville, KY, with her husband Stanley and son Brendan. She is available on an international basis to keynote, train and consult. This is her third book.

Learn more and contact Michele:

Info@MicheleShelton.com

MicheleShelton.com

LinkedIn.com/in/michele-lawlis-shelton-b0528420

Chapter Fourteen

TRACY STUCKRATH

"Diversity & Inclusion – What's Food Got to Do with It?"

At the same time that diversity, inclusion and employee well-being have become CEO-level issues for companies these past few years, the number of people (employees) who are following diets for various medical, religious and/or personal reasons has increased. As such, inclusivity and dietary needs now intertwine — indeed, the need to understand, respect and accommodate an employees' special diet in the workplace is a vital part of allowing them to bring their whole selves to work.

A few years ago at a convention, I attended a reception to kick off and promote LGBT inclusion within the meeting's industry. While the event was well-attended by people of different genders, race/ethnicity, generation, sexual orientation and sectors of the industry, and was a wonderful tribute to the LGBT community, I personally walked away feeling excluded … and hungry.

Yes, I'm saying I felt excluded because there was nothing for me to eat.

The hosts of the event didn't take the time to choose food items that provided for a variety of different needs, and the hotel failed to provide labeling for the food to communicate allergens, ingredients or dietary needs that the food met. Both of these decisions are subconscious ways of excluding some from fully participating and enjoying an event.

You might be thinking "go get food somewhere else," "pick around the food to eat what you can eat," or "I shouldn't have to accommodate everyone's needs." All could be valid statements, but when you're promoting inclusiveness and/or talking about someone's health, these statements are moot.

What if there is no other place to get something to eat? What if the person has an allergy where even a crumb of something will harm them? What if you tried to provide something for everyone?

Kristi has an allergy to both milk and corn, has celiac disease and follows a vegetarian diet. She notes that if she is exposed to wheat, her "lips end up with 'Edward Scissorhands' lesions," and she throws up if she eats corn. When asked about whether the management of her dietary needs has been easy or difficult at work or while traveling, she says there are a lot of packable meals and snack bars that she brings with her for situations like the example above. She no longer takes it personally when colleagues don't provide her with something she can safely eat, but she does take note of people who care enough to try and accommodate and, conversely, those who are ignorant of their lack of inclusion.

―――――――――――――

When we sit down at a table to enjoy a meal, we come together to meet as equals. We're able to look each other in the eye. We build trust. We build relationships. To be invited to dinner — literally or figuratively — is not doing anyone else a favor. It is meant to include us as part of a group.

So, when literally inviting someone to join you for a meal, you should not only provide them an opportunity to build a new relationship, but also a delicious meal that is also safe for them to eat. For the event mentioned above, which was about promoting inclusiveness within an industry, they neglected to ensure that people attending who had food allergies or religious requirements could find something they could eat, creating a level of exclusion. This was the opposite of what they intended.

When we sit down at a table to enjoy a meal, we come together to meet as equals. We're able to look each other in the eye. We build trust.

In the workplace, diversity and inclusion are now CEO-level issues that are being addressed on many fronts except, in a lot of instances, when it comes to food and beverage.

Last year, I reached out to Andrea, a vice president for talent and diversity at a large international communications company, to gain insight on how the company's policies on employee well-being, diversity and inclusion addressed the dietary needs of its employees in the company.

When we sat down, Andrea asked me to explain what I meant. I described a typical staff meeting where she might ask her assistant to order lunch for the group. The assistant will call a local sandwich shop or the company cafeteria to place the order with the standard turkey, roast beef and ham sandwiches with pasta salad, potato chips and pickles on the side. I explained, that without even thinking, the lunch excluded the members of her team who are vegetarian, vegan and/or are gluten-free, or who follow a religious-based diet.

At that moment, her eyes lit up. Andrea realized what I was saying and explained to me that in that scenario, she would actually be excluded herself because she is a diabetic vegetarian. While she could eat the chips and the pickle that came with the meal, neither of those are nutritious or acceptable lunch options for her.

Andrea then went on to describe that going down to the company cafeteria, she is unable able to eat the vegetable soup because it's made with chicken broth. This prompted her to ask if I'd go speak to the catering company that manages their cafeteria and ask them to make a change.

My response was that, as their client, the request to provide alternative options for employees (as well as clear labeling) would be more effective if the request came from the organization. If it's part of the company culture and policies, the catering company would need to adapt and provide options.

During our 45-minute conversation, it became increasingly apparent to Andrea that the dietary needs of employees are impacted in so many ways within the workplace and, given her leadership role, there were so many ways she could help change that.

Fortunately, not all employers are dropping the ball when it comes to inclusive food and beverage. Take, for example, my conversation with Elton, a chef at a large international technology company that provides free meals to all employees three times a day on each of its many campuses. I asked him how they accommodate the dietary needs of the employees. He said they take dietary needs very seriously. They make from scratch a variety of options that meet the needs of various food allergies and dietary restrictions. If, for example, they are serving beef tacos, they also make sure there are vegetarian, vegan, gluten-free and dairy-free options for everyone. They label every food that is served with the ingredients, down to the oil being used during the cooking process. And, if the food is not made from scratch, they read and provide any information from the packaged food they purchased (e.g., the graham crackers were made in a facility that also processes soy and tree nuts). Elton's company wants to be transparent about the food they are providing.

When I asked him where accommodating the dietary needs of employees falls within the company policies, he was perplexed. What policies? It is in the culinary manual that all chefs within the company follow. "We want the employees — and their guests — to be able to come to the cafeteria and the other food outlets on campus to find something safe and delicious to eat," he explained. As a chef to so many employees and guests, he says, "it just makes sense to be inclusive of everyone, right?"

INCLUSIVENESS IS ABOUT A WORK ENVIRONMENT OF TRUST AND INVOLVEMENT

The work environment where Elton works is inclusive. It also inspires and creates trust between the company and the employees.

Greg Harmeyer, CEO of TiER1 Performance, in an interview on the "Businesses that Care" podcast, says employers need to think holistically about getting the most from their employees, and this means allowing them to bring their whole selves to work. Someone's personal life comes to work with them and their work goes home with them. Employees need to be who they are and should be encouraged to be who they are, even at work.

These days, companies must recognize the whole person they are hiring and create a culture in which the company and the employees "trust, share and care about one another," says Harmeyer. It has to start from the top, and it needs to be "authentic and it should not be a contingent to get them to do work," he continues.

A Gallup study supports Harmeyer's comments — "the employee engagement elements most strongly linked to perceptions of inclusiveness are someone 'seems to care about me as a person' and 'my opinions seem to count.'"[1]

Think about a time that you've been left out and excluded in a social situation. How did that make you feel? Was it a friend, family member or a stranger who made you feel that way?

It's a common human experience, but it's not fun. It actually hurts.

When my friend Jill — who has been a vegetarian for more than 25 years — goes home for the holidays, she often finds bacon bits on all the of the food options. Her relatives say, "Oh, I forgot," or "I didn't think about it." Think about how that has made her feel, especially since they've known she has been a vegetarian this whole time. They didn't take the time to think about everyone they were serving.

The same can be said about food at work. When there is nothing safe or inclusive for someone to eat at an event — staff meeting, sales conference, employee picnic — they are being excluded from fully participating in that event and it can hurt. It can even be detrimental to work production.

Karen, who has allergies to milk, melon, avocado, squash, banana and cucumber, asks that there be options to for people with dietary restrictions when providing meals at work: "There are many other allergies out

---

1   "Using Employee Engagement to Build a Diverse Workforce," Rebecca Riffkin and Jim Harter, http://news.gallup.com/opinion/gallup/190103/using-employee-engagement-build-diverse-workforce.aspx

there and having confidence everyone can eat the meal provided is very compassionate."

Then there is Shirley, who doesn't often mention she has a wheat allergy and non-celiac gluten sensitivity because "generally it sets me apart around meal times … and I don't want to be seen as different." She also didn't tell her boss because she works at a food company and her job entails tasting the company product, and she didn't want to be restricted in her role or future roles within the company.

When there is nothing safe or inclusive for someone to eat at an event — staff meeting, sales conference, employee picnic — they are being excluded from fully participating in that event and it can hurt.

One Deloitte study shows that inclusion is not just about assembling diverse teams but also about connecting team members so that everyone is heard and respected.[2] And other research study by Deloitte comparing high-performing teams against lower-performing teams supports the view that people must feel included in order to speak up and fully contribute.[3]

2, 3   "Diversity and Inclusion: The Reality Gap," 2017 Global Human Capital Trends, Juliet Bourke, Stacia Garr, Ardie van Berkel, Jungle Wong, February 28, 2017.

FIVE STRATEGIES TO PROVIDE MORE INCLUSIVE MEALS IN THE WORKPLACE

So, how do you go about providing a more inclusive workplace as it relates to food and beverage in the workplace? Consider these five strategies:

1. Take a survey (can be anonymous) of your employees to ask them if they have any dietary needs. Let them know that, in an effort to provide a more inclusive food environment at work, you'd like to know if they have any dietary needs.

2. Because eating and all bodily functions were added as major life activities to the Americans with Disabilities Act with its 2008 amendment, I suggest asking this question to employees in two ways. First, ask if anyone has a medically necessary diet that requires them to eat in a specific way as to not harm them. And, second, ask if they have any dietary preferences that you can accommodate. See the image below or visit www.thrivemeetings.com/youatworksurvey.

3. Create a company policy on inclusion that includes employees' dietary needs as what completes a person's whole self.

4. When planning an event with food, select and provide a range of food that includes vegan/vegetarian, gluten-free, healthy, and kosher/halal options. Ensure all food is clearly labeled and/or either individually packaged or offered in a way that avoids cross-contamination. Ask participants if they have any needs that should be provided for when ordering. And, request the restaurant or caterer if they can provide alternative menus that can be shared with the attendees so they may choose their own meal.

5. Make sure you have an emergency care plan in case an employee has an allergic or medical reaction. Everyone in the company should

be made aware of the plan. Knowing and following the plan will help your employees feel less anxious and more in control of their health at work.

Learn more and educate your team about dietary needs. This builds confidence, helps advocate for your employees and allows your employees to trust your motives.

If you want to build a truly-inclusive workplace that encourages employees to bring their whole selves to work and engages them on all levels, you should be willing and able to offer food and beverage options that meet the needs of many. It could bring about a whole new level of education and engagement, and the results might very well be extraordinary.

EVENT REGISTRATION QUESTIONS

Step 1. Ask if your attendees have any ADA Disabilities that the meeting host should be aware of and provide accommodations.

ADA Disabilities

- [ ] Mobile
- [ ] Vision
- [ ] Auditory
- [x] Dietary Need
  (medically necessary; food allergies, celiac disease, diabetes)
- [ ] Other
  _____
- [ ] None

Step 2. If a person selects "Dietary Need," then ask them if their medically necessary dietary need is a food allergy, diabetes, celiac disease or other. If someone selects other, there should be a box for them to complete and/or the meeting host should contact them to discuss.

Medically Necessary Dietary Need

☑ Food Allergy

☐ Diabetes

☐ Celiac Disease or Non-Celiac Gluten Sensitivity

☐ Other _____

Step 3. If the person selects Food Allergy, allow them to select the food(s) that cause allergic reactions for them. The TOP 8 foods that cause 90 percent of all allergic reactions worldwide — eggs, wheat, milk, soy, shellfish, fish, tree nuts, peanuts — should, at a minimum be listed as shown below. The other foods on the list below are foods regulated by governments around the world as food allergens.

I will require immediate medical attention if I consume any of the foods checked below. (Please select all that apply.)

☐ Eggs	☐ Mollusks	☐ Buckwheat
☑ Wheat	☐ Gluten	☐ Peaches
☑ Milk	☐ Mustard	☐ Pork
☐ Soy	☐ Sesame	☐ Barley
☐ Crustaceans	☐ Lupin	☐ Bee Pollens
☐ Fish	☐ Celery	☐ Royal Jelly
☐ Tree Nuts	☐ Sulfites	☐ Other
☐ Peanuts	☐ Tomatoes	_____

Step 4. For those individuals who have food allergies, you should also ask how their allergy is triggered and if they carry epinephrine on them. Some people cannot be in a room with an allergen without it causing a reaction. Other may only experience reactions when they actually ingest the food. When ordering food, it is important to know if you must completely keep a food ingredient out of the menu completely.

My allergy is triggered by:

☑ Eating the food

☐ Touching the food

☐ Smelling (I can't be in the room with it)

☑ Is there treatment or accommodation you want us to be aware of to help mitigate your health and safety risks at the event?

☐ Please complete this emergency action plan for yourself

Step 5. The next question on your registration form should address whether attendees have any dietary preferences. This next box shows these options. Please know that some people eat vegan or vegetarian for medical reasons and may make a note of it on the previous question as well as here.

- ☑ **Vegetarian** (I eat eggs and milk, but no other animal products)
- ☐ **Vegan** (I do not eat any animal products of any kind)
- ☐ **Pescatarian** (I eat eggs, milk and seafood, but no other animal products)
- ☐ **Halal**
- ☐ **Kosher**
- ☐ **Gluten-Free** (I avoid gluten, but do not have celiac)
- ☐ **No Alcohol** (I do not drink or eat foods with alcohol)
- ☐ **No Pork** (I do not eat pork or items made with it)
- ☐ **No Red Meat** (I do not eat any red meat or items made with it)
- ☐ **Other** _____
- ☐ **None**

Step 6. If a person selects halal or kosher, a best practice is to find out if they require a certified halal or kosher meal. Some individuals follow strict practices at home, but may follow general guidelines when eating out.

- ☐ **Strict Kosher** (I require a meal prepared in a certified kosher kitchen; I will not eat off of the buffet)
- ☐ **Kosher** (I require a meal without pork, shellfish, or meat and dairy together; I can eat off of the buffet as long as it is labeled)
- ☐ **Strict Halal** (I require a meal prepared in a certified halal kitchen; I will not eat off of the buffet)
- ☐ **Halal** (I require a meal without pork and/or alcohol; I will eat from the buffet as long as it is labeled)
- ☑ **A vegetarian meal is acceptable**
- ☐ **A vegan meal is acceptable**

ABOUT THE AUTHOR

Tracy Stuckrath
CSEP, CMM, CHC

Tracy Stuckrath, founder and chief food officer of Thrive!, helps organizations worldwide understand how food and beverage affects risk, employee/guest experience, company culture and the bottom line.

As an award-winning event planner, international speaker, author, consultant and industry activist, she is passionate about inclusive food and beverage that satisfies everyone's dietary needs and leaves no one hungry at the table.

With more than 28 years' experience planning meetings and events, Tracy realized later in life the importance of food to both health and relationships. As one of 15 million Americans with food allergies, she has both personal and professional experience in managing dietary needs at meetings and at work.

Since 2008, Tracy has been working hard to build safer, more delicious, and inclusive food and beverage environment at events and in the workplace. For her work, she's been named a Top 25 Women in the Meetings Industry, 40 Over 40 Meeting Professional, Meetings Industry Change Maker, U.S. delegate to Slow Food's Terra Madre Salone del Gusto, Les Dames D'Escoffier inductee, and a Meetings Industry Trendsetter.

She's shared her passion for safe and inclusive food and beverage to audiences on five continents, and as a freelance writer for *Allergic Living* magazine, *The Meeting Professional*, *Meetings Today*, *Restaurant Informer*,

Plan Your Meetings, BizBash, Meetings & Conventions, MeetingsNet, Convene and *Special Events*.

Tracy is a graduate of North Carolina State University, holding a BA in Communications and Business. She spends her spare time taking her nieces and nephew on experience trips, and with her 96-year-old grandmother, parents and friends. This is her second book co-authoring experience; she was a featured author in the human resource anthology *Humans@Work*, the first @Work Series book, of which *You@Work* is a part.

Learn more and contact Tracy:

Tracy@thrivemeetings.com

Thrivemeetings.com

LinkedIn.com/in/tracystuckrath

Facebook.com/thrivemeetingsevents

Twitter.com/tstuckrath

404-242-0530

100% OF THE PUBLISHER PROCEEDS FROM THE AMAZON PAPERBACK SALES OF THIS BOOK WILL BENEFIT THE SHRM FOUNDATION

The SHRM Foundation is a values-based charity organization whose mission is to champion workforce and workplace transformation by providing research-based HR solutions for challenging inclusion issues facing current and potential employees, scholarships to educate and develop HR professionals to make change happen and opportunities for HR professionals to make a difference in their local communities. The SHRM Foundation is a 501(c)(3) nonprofit organizational affiliate of the Society for Human Resource Management.

Learn more at www.shrm.org/foundation.

SHRM
Foundation

Stay tuned for the next book in the @Work Series:

IMAGINATION@WORK:
SHIFTING BOUNDARIES IN THE
MODERN WORKPLACE

If you are an HR or OD expert with interest in being a contributing author for a future @Work anthology, please contact Cathy Fyock at 502-445-6539 or Cathy@CathyFyock.com.

@work
SERIES